Timed Reading
for Fluency

3

Timed Reading for Fluency 3

Paul Nation / Casey Malarcher

© 2017 Seed Learning, Inc.
7212 Canary Lane,
Sachse, TX, USA

Acquisitions Editor: Kelly Daniels
Content Editor: David Charlton
Copy Editor: Andrea Janzen
Design: Highline Studio

The authors would like to acknowledge Kelly Lee, Randy Lewis, and Joy Yongo for contributing material to this book.

http://www.seed-learning.com

ISBN: 978-1-9464-5269-6

10 9 8 7 6 5 4 3
22 21 20 19

Photo Credits

Timed Reading for Fluency

3

Paul Nation / Casey Malarcher

Seed Learning

Contents

Introduction / 6

Chapter 1 Sociology / 9

Reading 1 Should Kids Change Their Names? / 11
Reading 2 Does Wealth Affect Ethics? / 13
Reading 3 The Age for Marriage / 15
Reading 4 How Social Media Is Changing the World / 17
Reading 5 Homes Around the World / 19

Chapter 2 Technology / 21

Reading 6 Big Data and You / 23
Reading 7 The History of the Internet / 25
Reading 8 3D Printing / 27
Reading 9 The History of the Smartphone / 29
Reading 10 Virtual Reality / 31

Chapter 3 Geography / 33

Reading 11 Climate Change, Sea Changes / 35
Reading 12 Is Earth Running Out of Water? / 37
Reading 13 Glaciers / 39
Reading 14 The Yellowstone Caldera / 41
Reading 15 The Ring of Fire / 43

Chapter 4 History / 45

Reading 16 Castles in Europe / 47
Reading 17 The Pig War / 49
Reading 18 A Great Deal for the US / 51
Reading 19 The Terracotta Army / 53
Reading 20 The Brick Kingdom / 55

Chapter 5 Economics / 57

Reading 21	Supply and Demand	/ 59
Reading 22	The Minimum Wage	/ 61
Reading 23	How Monopolies Affect Economies	/ 63
Reading 24	The Job of Banks	/ 65
Reading 25	The Economic Fallacy of Free	/ 67

Chapter 6 Literature / 69

Reading 26	Should Books Be Free to Read Online?	/ 71
Reading 27	The Decline of the Printed Word	/ 73
Reading 28	Copyright Laws	/ 75
Reading 29	Banned Books	/ 77
Reading 30	The Language of Shakespeare	/ 79

Chapter 7 Space / 81

Reading 31	Earth's Moon	/ 83
Reading 32	Our Star, the Sun	/ 85
Reading 33	Living on Mars	/ 87
Reading 34	An Eye on Other Planets	/ 89
Reading 35	Water Power for Space Travel	/ 91

Chapter 8 People / 93

Reading 36	How to Succeed in Surfing	/ 95
Reading 37	Coming-of-Age Traditions	/ 97
Reading 38	Twin Studies	/ 99
Reading 39	Wonder, Study, and Learn!	/ 101
Reading 40	To Make Her Country Free	/ 103

Reading Speed Chart / 105

Introduction

A well-organized language course provides opportunities for learning through communicative activities involving listening, speaking, reading and writing, deliberate study, and fluency development. The fluency development part of a course should take about one-quarter of the course time, and there should be fluency development activities for each of the four skills of listening, speaking, reading, and writing.

This series of books focuses on fluency in reading. Fluency involves making the best use of what you already know. That comes from working with familiar vocabulary and grammar, and from practicing using them in a comfortable way without having to struggle.

Seven Requirements of Fluency Development:

1. Familiar Material

Material for fluency development must be known and familiar. It should not involve unfamiliar language items or content too far removed from what learners already know. This is because to become fluent, learners need to focus on using material they already know well, not on learning new vocabulary or grammar. This is why the texts in these books are grouped into topic areas so that learners can read several texts about very similar information. Their familiarity with the topic will help them increase their reading speed.

Contents

Introduction / 6

1 Sociology / 9
Reading 1 Should Kids Change Their Names? / 11
Reading 2 Does Wealth Affect Ethics? / 13
Reading 3 The Age for Marriage / 15
Reading 4 How Social Media Is Changing the World / 17
Reading 5 Homes Around the World / 19

2 Technology / 21
Reading 6 Big Data and You / 23
Reading 7 The History of the Internet / 25
Reading 8 3D Printing / 27
Reading 9 The History of the Smartphone / 29
Reading 10 Virtual Reality / 31

3 Geography / 33
Reading 11 Climate Change, Sea Changes / 35
Reading 12 Is Earth Running Out of Water? / 37
Reading 13 Glaciers / 39
Reading 14 The Yellowstone Caldera / 41
Reading 15 The Ring of Fire / 43

4 History / 45
Reading 16 Castles in Europe / 47
Reading 17 The Pig War / 49
Reading 18 A Great Deal for the US / 51
Reading 19 The Terracotta Army / 53
Reading 20 The Brick Kingdom / 55

5 Economics / 57
Reading 21 Supply and Demand / 59
Reading 22 The Minimum Wage / 61
Reading 23 How Monopolies Affect Economies / 63
Reading 24 The Job of Banks / 65
Reading 25 The Economic Fallacy of Free / 67

6 Literature / 69
Reading 26 Should Books Be Free to Read Online? / 71
Reading 27 The Decline of the Printed Word / 73
Reading 28 Copyright Laws / 75
Reading 29 Banned Books / 77
Reading 30 The Language of Shakespeare / 79

7 Space / 81
Reading 31 Earth's Moon / 83
Reading 32 Our Star, the Sun / 85
Reading 33 Living on Mars / 87
Reading 34 An Eye on Other Planets / 89
Reading 35 Water Power for Space Travel / 91

8 People / 93
Reading 36 How to Succeed in Surfing / 95
Reading 37 Coming-of-Age Traditions / 97
Reading 38 Twin Studies / 99
Reading 39 Wonder, Study, and Learn! / 101
Reading 40 To Make Her Country Free / 103

Reading Speed Chart / 105

2. Quantity of Practice

Another key requirement of a fluency development course is quantity of practice. Fluency develops by doing plenty of practice with easy material. That is why each book in this series contains a lot of reading texts. When learners have finished working through one book in the series, it is a good idea if they go back over the texts they have already read, trying to read them faster than they did the first time.

3. Controlled Vocabulary

Learners do not get fluent in reading by struggling through difficult texts with lots of unknown words. The books in this series are carefully written within a controlled vocabulary so that there is a minimum of unknown words. Words that might be unfamiliar to some learners are dealt with before the reading texts.

4. Limited Headwords

Book 1 is written within a vocabulary of 800 words, Book 2 within 1,100 words, Book 3 within 1,500 words, and Book 4 within 2,000 words.

5. Pressure to Go Faster

A fluency development course will work well if there is some pressure to go faster when using the language. This series of books uses timed readings. When the learners read, they measure how long it takes them to do the reading, and they keep a record of their reading speed. Their aim is to increase their speed until it gets close to 250 words per minute.

6. A Focus on Comprehension

Fluency in reading not only involves speed of word recognition, but also involves comprehension. This is why the texts in these books are followed by questions. There is no value in reading faster if there is a big drop in comprehension.

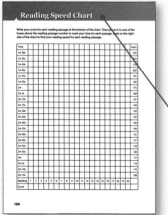

7. Graphs to Chart Progress

At the back of each book there is a graph where learners should enter their reading speed for each text and their comprehension score. The learners' goal should be to make their reading speed graph keep going up.

Chapter 1 Sociology

A **Look at the pictures. Circle the right words.**

1. The only way to cross the desert in the (average / southern) part of the country was by camel.

2. My grandfather built this treehouse when he was a (census / teenager).

3. Is it accurate to say that marriage is the beginning of (childhood / adulthood)?

4. The birth rate has decreased in some countries, but the worldwide population continues to (increase / decrease).

B **What do you think is the right answer? Check (✓) it.**

1. What do people tend to use more of today? ☐ Apps ☐ Tents
2. What does a census count? ☐ Candy in a bowl ☐ Number of people
3. What is knowledge of right and wrong? ☐ Ethics ☐ Social media
4. Who is a strong influence during childhood? ☐ The government ☐ Friends
5. Why is the number of marriages declining? ☐ A decrease in importance ☐ An increase in products

C **Work with a classmate. Try to write three ideas for each box.**

	Childhood	Adulthood
Advantages		
Disadvantages		

D **Add a part from the "First" box to a part from the "Last" box to make eight words or phrases. Write the words and phrases below.**

First				Last		
adult	app	child	de	ern	ager	crease (X2)
in	social	south	teen	hood (X2)	store	media

1. _____   3. _____   5. _____   7. _____

2. _____   4. _____   6. _____   8. _____

Proper Nouns to Know

Study these words that you will find in the readings for this chapter.

Bagaboa   Bedouin   Canada   Facebook

Gobi Desert   Greenland   Instagram   Inuit

Middle East   Mongolian   North Africa   Philippines

Spain   Twitter   WhatsApp

Should Kids Change Their Names?

Some people like their names, but others are not happy with them. Children are named by their parents. Many times, these names have an important meaning for their parents. Some parents name their children after a member of their family. For example, children may be named after a grandmother or an uncle. Parents may also give children

5 names that will make children feel like they have a certain goal. For example, some children are named after famous kings or queens. At times, there are parents who have named their children something unusual. For example, there have been children named Apple or Peace. Since children do not get to pick their names, they may feel bad. They may want to change their names. As children grow up, they may find a new name that seems to

10 fit them better than the one their parents gave them. Should these children be allowed to change their names?

Some people say children should be able to change their names, especially if their names are unusual. This is because children with very unusual names are sometimes treated badly by others.

15 Other children may make fun of a child with an unusual name. Some children's names are spelled very differently from how they sound. This also causes problems for such children. They may not like the member of the family they are named after, or they may not agree with their parents about certain ideas related to their names.

20 Other people say that children should not be able to change their names. This is largely because children change a lot as they grow. One name may seem good during childhood, but then may not seem very good in adulthood. Name changing again as an adult leads to confusion all around. Children may also be easily influenced by their friends. Children who only listen to their friends do not always make good decisions. Parents, not

25 friends, should be the major influence in a child's life. Since parents give their children a lot of love and care, they may feel hurt if the child wants to change his or her name.

Time

Word Count 350 words

Comprehension Questions

Circle the right answer.

1. This reading is about
   a. children who have changed their names and why.
   b. why children change their names.
   c. whether children should be able to change their names.

2. Which of the following is NOT mentioned as how parents pick names?
   a. They want the child's name to sound funny.
   b. They name a child after a relative.
   c. They name a child with a special goal in mind.

3. The writer says that children may not like unusual names because
   a. they know that they will grow up.
   b. some people will think they are special.
   c. people sometimes will treat them badly.

4. Some people say children should not be able to change their names because
   a. people make fun of their unusual names.
   b. children are easily influenced by their friends.
   c. some people in the family do not like the name.

5. Parents can feel bad when children want to change their names because
   a. they want children to have unusual names.
   b. they love and take care of their children.
   c. they think their children are like adults.

Score _____

Extra Practice

Choose the word or phrase with a similar meaning as the underlined part.

1. A good teacher can <u>influence</u> students to make good choices.   guide / pick

2. <u>Certain</u> names can be given to both boys and girls.   Better / Some

3. During most of my <u>childhood</u>, I lived in Canada.   vacation / young years

4. Kids look forward to <u>adulthood</u> when they finish schooling.   being older / the afternoon

5. My dad goes by a short form of his name <u>since</u> his real name is long.   because / if

Does Wealth Affect Ethics?

Would you lie to get $50? Would you lie to get $50 for a friend, not yourself? These are some questions that researchers ask in ethics studies. Money has always caused problems between people, but researchers wanted to know if money affects a person's ethics. They did different kinds of experiments and studied rich and poor people. Some studies were about how people felt about money, and others were about pretending to be a richer person.

One interesting study was about people who drove very nice cars and people who did not. Researchers watched how rich people acted when they were driving. They also watched how poorer people acted. Another study was about candy. In this study, researchers told a person that a bowl of candy was for children in the next room. The person was allowed to take some candy before the bowl was given to the children. Each person in the study was told to think about being rich or being very poor. Researchers also did a study in which people imagined getting money according to their actions. Researchers told people they could get $50 if they got a certain score in a game. Then they told other people their friends would get $50 if they got a certain score in the game.

These studies showed some surprising things about people and ethics. The people with very nice cars tended not to be very careful when they were driving, and they sometimes cut off other drivers. The people who thought about being rich tended to take more candy from the bowl. The richer people also tended to lie about their score in the game to get the money. Researchers found that richer people tended not to lie for friends. Were the findings any different for poorer people in any of these studies? Poorer drivers tended to be kinder and more careful drivers. Poorer people tended not to take much candy from the bowl. They also tended not to lie about their scores. But poorer people did lie when they were told that their friends would get something good.

Time _____

Word Count   350 words

Circle the right answer.

1. This reading is about
   a. why richer people are better than poor people in ethics studies.
   b. how the ethics of rich and poor people tend to be different.
   c. research on the ethics of drivers and how much money they have.

2. Researchers watched people driving to find out
   a. if rich people and poor people acted in certain ways.
   b. if richer people have nicer cars than poorer people have.
   c. if rich people cut off poor drivers more often than other drivers.

3. Which of the following is NOT mentioned as part of a study?
   a. People were told they could take candy from a bowl.
   b. Researchers watched rich people and poor people driving cars.
   c. People watched researchers pretend they were rich.

4. The writer says that
   a. poorer people tended to be more careful drivers.
   b. poorer people tended to take more candy from the bowl.
   c. poorer people tended to lie to their friends.

5. Richer people tended to
   a. lie more often about driving nicer cars.
   b. eat more candy when they are driving.
   c. not respect others while driving.

Score _____

Extra Practice

Write the right word in each blank to complete the summary.

candy	ethics	experiments	kindly	tended

Researchers wanted to see how money affected people's 1. _____. They asked some rich and poor people to help with their 2. _____. In one study, they had people think about being rich or poor and then asked them to take 3. _____ from a bowl. It was interesting to find that people 4. _____ to take more candy when they thought about being rich. People who were poor or thought about being poor tended to act more 5. _____.

The Age for Marriage

Marriage is an old and common custom in all cultures. Most marriages are between two adults, although some countries allow children to wed. And in the United States, studies show that the average marriage age of adults is changing.

In the United States, records of couples getting married have been kept since the country's beginning. Those records are not complete, but they can give us an idea of how old people were when they got married. People started keeping better records in 1880. In that year, the government began to take a census of families. After that time, the average age of marriage was more clearly understood by researchers and the government.

From the information that is available about marriages in the US, some interesting trends have been found. In the 1600s, women usually married as teenagers or in their early twenties. The average age for men was around 25. By the end of the 1800s, the marriage age for women had increased, but for men, it had stayed about the same. The 1880 census showed that the average age for men was 26.5. The average age for women was 23.0. In the next census ten years later, the numbers were 23.6 for women and 27.6 for men.

Surprisingly, into the 1900s, the average age for marriage began to decrease. The marriage age for men and women decreased to its lowest point in 1960. For men, the typical marriage age was around 23, and for women it was 20. But, since 1960, the average marriage age has been rising again. By 1990, the age at which men typically wed was again around 27 and for women 25. And it is still going up. Recent studies show that men are now getting married at 29 and women at 27.

For more than 400 years, the average marriage age in the US has gone up and down. But these latest average ages are the highest ever. And because they are continuing to rise, some people are worried. They are afraid that the numbers mean that marriage is becoming less important.

Time _____

Word Count 350 words

Comprehension Questions

Circle the right answer.

1. This reading is about
   a. the earliest marriage age for American women.
   b. the average marriage age in the world.
   c. the average marriage age in the US.

2. In the United States, marriage records have been kept
   a. since before 1800.
   b. since the mid 1800s.
   c. since the 1960s.

3. Which of the following is NOT true according to the article?
   a. Marriage is common to all cultures.
   b. Child marriages are very common.
   c. We can learn about families through a census.

4. The marriage age was lowest for men and women in
   a. 1960.
   b. 1600.
   c. 2000.

5. Some people are worried about the increasing marriage age today because
   a. they think governments will stop taking censuses.
   b. they say records are being taken incorrectly.
   c. they are afraid marriage is becoming unimportant.

 Score _____

Extra Practice

Choose the word or phrase with a similar meaning as the underlined part.

1. My mom and dad <u>got married</u> when they were young.   wed / separated

2. Marriage is a <u>custom</u> found in nearly every culture.   government / tradition

3. <u>Governments</u> record information about families during   Teenagers / Leaders
   each census.

4. The <u>average</u> marriage age in the US is higher than ever.   common / unusual

5. The <u>couple</u> plans to marry after they both graduate college.   pair / group

How Social Media Is Changing the World

Facebook is a social media app that allows people to connect with each other. Facebook, created in 2004, is by far the most popular social media site so far. In fact, as of 2016, there were over 1.6 billion Facebook users around the world. In total, there are about 2 billion people
5　who use any type of social media. Before 2020, this number is expected to grow to 2.5 billion people. With so many people connecting online around the world, social media has changed our lives a lot in recent years.

First, social media brings people closer together. Families
10　who live far from each other can have conversations and share pictures with each other on social media. Strangers who don't know each other can talk about similar interests. Even people who live in different countries can connect as if they were sitting in the same living room.

Second, almost every business uses social media to tell customers about their
15　services or products. The power of social media comes from the fact that so many people use it. In addition, social media sites record a lot of information about a person and the things he or she likes. Facebook is set up in such a way that only the ads that a person would be interested in are shown on his or her page. Not only can people see products, but they can also "like" the products and offer reviews on them. The more "likes" a product
20　has, the more likely others are going to buy it. This is why many businesses now consider social media sites as important factors affecting sales.

Third, social media has increased the voice of the people. For example, through pictures and video, people can now put their own news and ideas on the internet. No longer is the media in control of what kind of information is reported. People can now tell millions of
25　others what they think about events in the news. With text, videos, and pictures, social media is able to influence public opinion on just about any event reported in the news.

Word Count 350 words

Time

Comprehension Questions

Circle the right answer.

1. This reading is about
   a. different types of social media.
   b. how to use social media.
   c. social media's influence today.

2. What is social media?
   a. Websites and apps that allow us to share information
   b. Television and radio stations
   c. News that is made available online

3. The writer thinks social media
   a. makes people feel more alone.
   b. brings people closer together.
   c. is bad for the relationship of friends.

4. The writer says most businesses
   a. are not interested in social media.
   b. think social media hurts their business.
   c. use social media to tell people about products and services.

5. Who can make news available through social media?
   a. Anyone
   b. No one
   c. Only people working in media

 Score _____

Extra Practice

Write the right word in each blank to complete the summary.

billion	connect	influencing	app	products

Social media is changing the way people 1. _____ with each other. In fact, over a(n) 2. _____ people are using Facebook! This makes the 3. _____ a useful way for people to share ideas. In addition, businesses are able to use social media as a way to sell their 4. _____. When people talk about ideas and products using such apps, social media becomes a powerful tool for 5. _____ public opinion.

Homes Around the World

When you hear the word "home," you probably think of the place you are living in right now. Maybe it is an apartment, a single house, or a two-story house. Maybe it is made of wood or stone. You may think houses are rather normal buildings, but some houses around the world are rather unique!

5 　The Bedouin people of the Middle East and North Africa live in interesting homes. The Bedouin people live in the desert, and they move around without staying to live in one place very long. So, they live in tents that are made of animal hair. The tents are easy to put up and take down when they move from place to place. In a similar way, a group of Mongolian people of the Gobi Desert also live in tents rather than buildings. These homes,
10 called "ger" homes, are also made of animal hair, but they are round instead of square like Bedouin tents.

Before people made the first tents, they lived in caves. Some people in the southern part of Spain live in caves today, too! They call these cave homes "cuebas." These caves keep the house cool during the summer and warm during the winter.

15 　Another type of home is the "igloo" used by the Inuit people of Canada and Greenland. Igloos are normally made of ice and snow. The igloo protects the people from the wind as well as keeps them warm. In fact, the temperature inside an igloo can even reach 16° C just from body heat alone.

The Bagabao people of the Philippines used to live in what may be a childhood
20 dream for some—a treehouse! These treehouses were built so that the people could watch for enemies and protect themselves from wild and dangerous animals. In addition, the people could stay cool in their treehouses during the hot summer season. Although the Bagabao people don't live in these treehouses anymore, they still use things like them for resting and for meeting people.

25 　If you ever get the chance, be sure to check out different homes of different cultures!

Time

Word Count 350 words

Comprehension Questions

Circle the right answer.

1. This reading is about
   a. where the best place to live is.
   b. different types of homes.
   c. how to build a house.

2. Which of the following is what the Bedouin used to make their tents?
   a. Animal hair
   b. Parts of plants
   c. Sand

3. The writer says that the "cuebas" in Spain are like
   a. cold houses.
   b. underground houses.
   c. treehouses.

4. An igloo can be kept warm by
   a. a heater.
   b. a fire.
   c. body heat.

5. The writer says that the people who used to live in treehouses are from
   a. North Africa.
   b. the Philippines.
   c. Mongolia.

 Score _____

Extra Practice

Choose the word or phrase with a similar meaning as the underlined part.

1. Wind, rain, and snow may influence what type of homes people live in.   Weather / Culture

2. Caves are warm in the winter and cool in the summer.   Small tents / Big holes

3. Igloos are unique to people living in the far north.   Ice houses / Treehouses

4. Living in tents rather than stone buildings makes it easier to move around.   in addition / instead of

5. Houses protect people from weather, animals, and enemies.   friends / strangers

Technology

Chapter 2

A Match two phrases with each type of technology.

a. combines a phone and computer
b. gives access to websites
c. may have a headset with headphones
d. creates objects in layers
e. can make jewelry
f. needs sensors
g. is a handheld device
h. needs a network connection

1. A smartphone: _____ and _____

2. Virtual reality: _____ and _____

3. The internet: _____ and _____

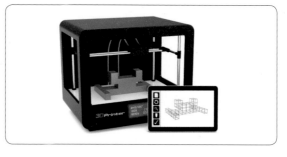

4. A 3D printer: _____ and _____

B Match the word with the right definition.

1. data _____
2. predict _____
3. laser _____
4. keyboard _____
5. combine _____

a. a device used for typing on computers
b. to put together
c. light in a focused form with a lot of energy
d. to say or guess what the future will be
e. information that a computer uses, usually in 0s and 1s

C Talk with a classmate. How often does he or she use each type of technology?

	Every day	Sometimes	Never
1. A smartphone	☐	☐	☐
2. A wi-fi network	☐	☐	☐
3. A laser printer	☐	☐	☐
4. A computer keyboard	☐	☐	☐
5. A virtual reality headset	☐	☐	☐

D Read the clues. Then use the words in the box to complete the puzzle.

access	device	headphones	jewelry	keyboard
laser	layer	sensor	smartphone	virtual

Across

2. You type on a ____.
3. Many women wear ____.
5. A small electronic machine
9. A phone combined with a computer
10. You can ____ the internet by a network.

Down

1. You use ____ to listen to music.
4. One level of a stack or pile
6. ____ reality
7. Light used to send data
8. A device that can see, hear, feel, etc.

Big Data and You

Big data is a lot of sets of information that are put together so they can be used by a computer program. The computer program looks for different kinds of answers or patterns in the data. Big data can have different kinds of

5 information from many sources, such as information that comes from schools, social media sites, companies, and governments. One set of data can have people's names and addresses. Another set can have what they like, where they go to school, and how much time they spend on the computer.

10 Big data can be used in many ways. The government uses it to understand how many people travel on buses or trains. This information is then used to make bus or train systems better. Some schools use big data to understand which children may need extra help in class. The teachers can then give certain students more help or support so those students can succeed in school. Companies use big data, too. It

15 helps them understand who buys their products. For example, one company uses weather data to see when people eat the most ice cream.

Big data can be used for good reasons. Some hospitals use big data to predict if a baby who is born too early will get sick. The hospital can then take extra steps to take care of that baby so he or she does not get sick. Big data can also be used for bad reasons. It can

20 be used to predict which kinds of people are likely to break the law or hurt others, even if they have not done anything wrong.

How can big data be used for good and bad things? It is because the computer programs used to look at big data and understand it are written by people. People think a certain way. Because they think a certain way, they build a model of those ideas. These

25 ideas are then used to look at the data. Sometimes, these ideas are helpful for people or businesses. Other times, bad ideas can cause problems for certain groups of people.

Time _____

Word Count 350 words

Comprehension Questions

Circle the right answer.

1. This reading is about
   a. how data is controlled by governments and companies.
   b. what big data is and how it is used.
   c. where important data is collected and stored.

2. The writer says that big data
   a. can be used for both good and bad reasons.
   b. is put together by governments to help hospitals.
   c. is not very useful for businesses.

3. Which of the following is NOT mentioned about computer programs?
   a. They are written by people.
   b. They can be used to create big data.
   c. They can have good or bad ideas in them.

4. One good thing about big data is how
   a. it helps control social media.
   b. it shows who will break the law.
   c. it helps babies in hospitals.

5. One company uses weather information to
   a. know when people will visit the hospital.
   b. understand when people will want ice cream.
   c. find out who rides the bus or train.

 Score _____

Extra Practice

Write the right word in each blank to complete the summary.

helpful	programs	information	government	patterns

Big data is a collection of lots of 1. _____ about people. Computer programs use this information to find answers or 2. _____. Big data is used by the 3. _____, schools, companies, and hospitals. It can be very 4. _____ because it can tell them about how people behave. It helps them know how to make 5. _____ better so that they can help more people.

ONLINE

The History of the Internet

The ideas about computers and connecting them together are not new. Some people were writing about them in the 1800s. However, in those early days of the computer age, there was no way to build a computer.

The first computers were made in the 1940s. However, most people did not have
5   computers when they first came out. This is because the very first computers were very large and expensive. Computers later became smaller and easier to buy.

People wanted to connect the computers so they could talk to each other and share information. The first time computers were able to work together using a special kind of network technology was in 1965. A network connects computers so they can talk to each
10 other and share information. The two computers that talked to each other in the 60s were at a university. In 1969, the ARPANET was one of the first networks made.

In the 1970s, people started to connect smaller networks together. This started to create a very large network of computers. These networks and computers were typically owned by governments and universities. One of the early goals of these networks was to
15 build a way to share information that was useful. If one part of the network was broken, people could still send and receive information on other parts. In 1981, the US government made it easier for more people to use ARPANET. A special group was then set up to help name new internet sites. However, it was not until 1989 that the World Wide Web—the internet as we know it—was created. It was created by a man named Tim Berners-Lee. He
20 wanted to make it easier for people to talk with each other and share ideas. ARPANET was very old by that time, and the government stopped using it in 1990.

The internet that most people know today is full of websites. In 1993, there were around 600 websites. Now, there are over one billion websites, and this number keeps increasing. As long as people want to share information, the
25 internet will keep growing.

Word Count   350 words

Time

Comprehension Questions

Circle the right answer.

1. This reading is about
    a. the history of ARPANET.
    b. how the internet was created.
    c. who put together the first networks.

2. Most people did not have the first computers because
    a. they were too expensive.
    b. they were too old.
    c. they were small and cheap.

3. Which of the following is NOT true about the internet?
    a. People started to connect computers together to make networks.
    b. The World Wide Web was made in the 1800s.
    c. ARPANET was used to share information.

4. The first people to use ARPANET
    a. used the 600 websites that were part of the World Wide Web.
    b. named the different websites on the internet.
    c. were from the government and universities.

5. One of the reasons for creating bigger computer networks was so that
    a. universities and governments could create more websites.
    b. if part of one was broken, people could still share information.
    c. Tim Berners-Lee could then share information with other countries.

 Score _____

Extra Practice

Choose the word or phrase with a similar meaning as the underlined part.

1. A <u>network</u> of computers can share information with each other.   group / goal
2. <u>Universities</u> were one of the first to use networks.   Artists / Schools
3. The <u>internet</u> is full of information and websites.   technology / web
4. The internet is a useful tool to <u>connect</u> people and share ideas.   join / receive
5. Researchers find more <u>information</u> about their ideas through experiments.   data / pages

3D Printing

Printing is one invention that has changed the modern world. In 1440, Gutenberg invented the printing press. This allowed books to be printed quickly. People no longer had to re-write important letters or books by hand. Since the invention of the printing press, many other forms of printing technology have come about. For example, screen printing, the
5 ability to print on clothes, was invented in 1910. Laser printing was invented in 1969. The latest invention is 3D printing, with the first 3D printer invented in 1984.

3D printing is a method of creating objects from a computer drawing. 3D printing uses materials such as different plastics to create objects. The 3D printer builds the object by adding layer after layer of the material until it finishes building the object.

10 3D printing's most useful purpose may be in the field of health. Doctors and hospitals now use 3D printing for medical purposes. No two people have exactly the same body parts. 3D printing could build medical objects that are specific to each person. In fact, it is already possible to build small, personal devices to help people's hearing and even teeth or small parts to go in teeth! The technology to use a 3D printer to "print" living cells is beginning as well.
15 Once the ability to "print" living cells is fully developed, it could be used to build skin, bones, and other body parts. This will help sick people as well as further medical research. However, the technology needed to reach this stage will take at least ten to twenty more years.

While 3D printing has a promising future for doctors and hospitals, the technology is also already being used today to make small models of houses and jewelry. In addition,
20 families with their own 3D printers in their homes can build fun objects such as toys. Artists are using 3D printers to create works of art, and sweet shops are even using these printers to print chocolate candies!

A 3D printer can take any drawing and build
25 it. That means the ability to make different objects using 3D printing has no end!

 Time _____

Word Count   350 words

Comprehension Questions

Circle the right answer.

1. This reading is about
   a. the history of printing.
   b. how 3D printing works and its uses.
   c. the inventor of 3D printing.

2. The writer says that a 3D printer creates objects from
   a. a computer drawing.
   b. one's thoughts.
   c. a photograph.

3. 3D printers create objects by
   a. adding layers on top of each other.
   b. adding colors in different stages.
   c. using heat to shape material.

4. Which of the following is NOT mentioned as an object a 3D printer has made?
   a. Toys
   b. Chocolate
   c. Phones

5. The writer says that the most useful purpose for 3D printing is in
   a. the field of medicine.
   b. making buildings and furniture.
   c. the field of fashion and design.

Score _____

Extra Practice

Write the right word in each blank to complete the summary.

chocolate	layers	medical	object	inventions

Printing is one of the most important 1. _____ in the modern world. The newest form of printing is 3D printing, which takes a computer image and makes it into a(n) 2. _____. The object is made when the printer takes material and starts to put it together in 3. _____. 3D printing will be useful for 4. _____ purposes as it will allow parts to be made that match a person's unique body. But it's not all serious work. Fun things like 5. _____ candy and jewelry can be made with 3D printing, too!

The History of the Smartphone

A smartphone is a phone that combines things like a phone, clock, camera, and computer into one small device. It can make regular calls like a phone, but it can also access the internet. Using internet apps, smartphones can play music, take pictures and videos, and check the weather in cities all around the world. But how did the age of
5   smartphones begin?

In 1992, the company IBM created the first smartphone. It was a phone that included a program for writing notes to remember things. It also had a program for showing people dates and times of scheduled events. This early smartphone could send emails as well. However, this phone never became very popular. For one thing, it was
10   too expensive for many people to want to buy one.

Other companies then started to work on new phone technology. Companies such as Nokia and Ericsson next introduced their smartphones to the market. In fact, it was the Ericsson company that created the word "smartphone" in 1997.
15   However, these smartphones also met with limited success.

In 1999, the Blackberry was introduced. This was the first smartphone that was widely used by phone users. The Blackberry was a phone with a keyboard that made sending text messages and emails, as well as using the internet, easy. The Blackberry was popular with people working in business or in technology. But regular phone users still didn't buy many of them.
20   In 2007, Apple introduced the iPhone. Not long after that, in 2008, Google introduced the Android phone to the world. These new smartphones from Apple and Google were marketed to all phone users. The goal was to make the smartphone easy to use and something everyone would want. Just as hoped, less than 10 years later, there were over 2 billion smartphone users. In addition, the number of users is expected to grow to more
25   than 6 billion by the year 2020. Not only is it safe to say that smartphones are taking over the world, there will soon be a time when people can't remember when phones only made calls.

Word Count 350 words

⏱ Time _____

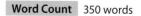

Comprehension Questions

Circle the right answer.

1. This reading is about

    a. what smartphones can do.

    b. who invented smartphones.

    c. how smartphones developed.

2. The company that made the first smartphone was

    a. Apple.

    b. Ericsson.

    c. IBM.

3. The company that created the word "smartphone" was

    a. Ericsson.

    b. Google.

    c. Nokia.

4. The writer says that the Blackberry was mainly for

    a. young people in university.

    b. people in business and technology.

    c. doctors and nurses.

5. The writer thinks most people will

    a. lose interest in the smartphone soon.

    b. own a smartphone soon.

    c. not need phones at all soon.

 Score _____

Extra Practice

Choose the word or phrase with a similar meaning as the underlined part.

1. A smartphone <u>combines</u> the jobs of a phone, camera, and computer.   mixes / expects

2. Blackberry's keyboard made sending <u>messages</u> and emails easier.   goals / texts

3. There is an app on my phone for making notes about my <u>day's plan</u>.   schedule / success

4. iPhones and Android phones are made to <u>market</u> to all phone users.   buy / sell

5. Smartphones are so <u>widely</u> used that there are already 2.1 billion users.   commonly / far

Virtual Reality

Virtual reality is a kind of technology that uses computers and programs to make a movie or game look and feel like it is real. Some people own a virtual reality game system. A number of these systems use cameras. You can also buy a special device to wear on your head. These devices have sensors on them. While you are watching the program inside

5 the device, these sensors and cameras are watching you. They watch how your head, eyes, and body move. They use this information to move around the pictures you see inside the device.

Some people also use special headphones with the device. The headphones have sensors on them. This information tells the headphones how to change the sound so it

10 seems more real to you. By combining the special viewing devices and headphones, a player can see and hear a virtual game space more like a real place.

You can also use special clothes that go over your hands and chest to feel like you are in the game. These clothes are filled with sensors. The sensors tell the game how you are moving. Then the game sends information to the clothes to do something. When you pick

15 up a ball in the game, you might feel like something is pressing on your hand.

Many kinds of virtual reality programs are used to make video games. However, virtual reality is being used for much more than just games. Governments use virtual reality to train some kinds of workers and soldiers. Then the workers and soldiers can practice what to do in different situations they might meet. In the business world, people

20 who want to see what a house or building might look like before it is built can look at it using virtual reality.

However, virtual reality does have some problems. While the virtual reality program watches your movements, it sometimes does not change the picture you see fast enough. Because it does

25 not change the picture or sound quickly, your body feels that there is a problem. This is why virtual reality can make some people sick.

Time

Word Count 350 words

Comprehension Questions

Circle the right answer.

1. This reading is about

    a. how virtual reality works and what it can do.

    b. virtual reality and its uses for government workers.

    c. how headphones and headsets are used in video games.

2. The writer says that virtual reality

    a. can make people sick.

    b. is used in schools.

    c. makes things less real.

3. Which of the following is NOT mentioned as a use of virtual reality?

    a. Looking at a house before it is built

    b. Helping people who are sick

    c. Government training

4. Virtual reality games use sensors to

    a. play the video game for the person.

    b. watch how you move your body and head.

    c. record a player's environment.

5. The writer talks about special clothes because

    a. they can help the person not get sick.

    b. they use special cameras.

    c. they can make the game feel more real.

 Score _____

Extra Practice

Write the right word in each blank to complete the summary.

headphones	device	sensors	soldiers	reality

    Virtual 1. _____ can make movies or games look and feel as if they are real. In virtual reality 2. _____ and cameras watch how a person's head and eyes move. This information is used to change the picture that a person sees through the 3. _____. Clothes and 4. _____ with sensors can make the experience more life-like. Virtual reality is not just for fun, though; it is also used to train 5. _____ in how to be prepared for serious situations.

Geography

A **Look at the pictures. Write the right words in the blanks.**

caldera	climate	crystals	eruption
glaciers	steam	surface	western

1. During a(n) _____, liquid rock flows from the volcano's _____.

2. Layers of tightly packed snow _____ will, over time, form _____.

3. The geysers of Yellowstone, a park in the _____ part of the US, shoot hot water and _____ into the air.

4. Some places on the _____ of the earth near oceans may be flooded due to _____ change.

B **Read the sentences. Circle True or False.**

1. We can only save water if people stop taking showers.   True   False
2. Moving tectonic plates cause earthquakes.   True   False
3. Solid water crystals form when temperatures are above 0°C.   True   False
4. Many volcanoes in Eastern Europe erupt every year.   True   False
5. You can see your face reflected in the water of a slow stream.   True   False

C Work with a group of classmates. Try to name one place for each of the following.

Name of Place

1. An eastern country   _____

2. A place with glaciers   _____

3. A place with hot springs or geysers   _____

4. A place where fresh water meets salt water   _____

5. A volcano that erupted in the past   _____

D Use the words in the box to complete the puzzle.

| caldera | climate | eastern | erupt | glacier | steam | tectonic | tightly |

1. The top of a volcano

2. A very big ice rock

3. Not loosely; very securely

4. Water as hot gas

5. The opposite of western

6. _____ plates of the earth

7. To explode, like a volcano

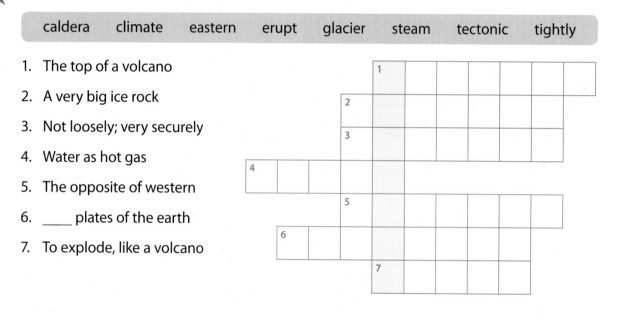

➤ The secret word: _____

Proper Nouns to Know

Study these words that you will find in the readings for this chapter.

Alaska   Aleutian Islands   Antarctica   Asia

Chile   Ferdinand Magellan   Hawaii   New Zealand

North America   Pacific Ocean   Portugal   South America

Wyoming   Yellowstone National Park

Climate Change, Sea Changes

Climate change is having a strong effect on areas of the world. Other than causing terrible storms in some places or periods of no rain for months at a time in other places, climate change has affected the temperature of the sea near land. When the temperature of the sea changes, this affects sea animals living in that area. People who make their living
5 in some way from the sea will have a hard time as the sea animals begin to die off. On top of this, in very cold areas, higher temperatures are causing glaciers to melt, which is causing sea levels around the world to rise.

Rising sea levels are a big problem. As areas of land beside the sea go under the water, the animals that used to live in these areas are forced to find new homes. Fresh
10 water lakes located near the shores of seas also become filled with salt water. In addition to these lakes, certain lands that are normally wet but still above sea level become flooded. These lands are important to the environment because they can help take out some kinds of poisons from water. They can also slow down or stop flooding of dry land above them. Due to climate change, some places that did not experience floods before, like farms far
15 from the sea, now get flooded with water. Even areas that regularly experience floods and were prepared for them now have larger and more dangerous floods.

While climate change affects the natural world, it also has a big effect on how people live. For example, when the sea level rises and the salt water moves higher up on the land, it can go into
20 the ground and get into areas where people get the fresh water they drink. Water from the sea is bad for cars, trucks, and boats. Bridges and roads can also be hurt by water from the sea. The walls people build to keep water out of cities and towns are in trouble, too.
25 Some of these walls may not be high enough to keep water out anymore.

 Time

Word Count 350 words

Comprehension Questions

Circle the right answer.

1. This reading is about
    a. how seas are important to the environment.
    b. how climate change affects areas by the sea.
    c. why some people are not worried about climate change.

2. The writer says that
    a. land and fresh water are affected by sea water.
    b. the land around seas is not affected by flooding.
    c. as glaciers melt, sea levels go down.

3. Which of the following is NOT mentioned as something that is affected by sea water?
    a. Bridges, trucks, and cars
    b. The places where people get fresh water
    c. Terrible storms

4. Lands that are normally wet are important because they
    a. are higher than the walls around cities.
    b. have fresh water that people drink.
    c. take out some poisons in water.

5. The writer says that
    a. flooding in areas by seas is not common.
    b. climate change makes floods more dangerous.
    c. some areas do not experience climate change.

 Score _____

Extra Practice

Choose the word or phrase with a similar meaning as the underlined part.

1. Climate change can cause serious problems in the sea and on land.   Storm / Weather
2. When glaciers melt, sea levels rise.   ice mountains / igloos
3. The water of the Nile River and Amazon River is fresh.   without salt / salty
4. The heavy spring rains caused floods that damaged many homes.   high water / walls
5. Temperatures that are not normal affect animals living in the area.   strange / usual

Is Earth Running Out of Water?

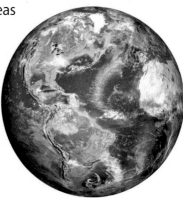

When we look at a picture of Earth from space, there are areas of green, blue, and white. Most people will recognize that the green is land, the blue is water, and the white is clouds. Taken as a whole, Earth is mainly blue. That is because of the amount of
5   water it has that covers the surface. In fact, Earth is often called the "Blue Planet" because of this. Not only does Earth appear blue because of the water, but there does not seem to be any other planet that has as much surface water in liquid form as Earth does. That is what makes Earth special.

10   So, how much of Earth is water? About 71% of Earth's surface is covered in water. Of that 71%, the oceans hold 96.5% of the water. This water found in oceans is all salt water. The remaining 3.5% of the water is fresh water, which can be found in lakes, rivers, glaciers, and in the ground. Fresh water is what people use for farming, raising animals, drinking, and daily activities such as taking showers and washing clothes or dishes.

15   Does the amount of water stay the same? For the most part, yes. Water on Earth is part of a closed system. That is, water is always moving and changing forms between ice, liquid, and gas. The form of the water changes all the time, but the total amount of water on Earth remains the same.

If Earth is not necessarily running out of water, why are people worried? Why do we
20   need to be concerned about saving water? First, humans can only use fresh water, which is only 3.5% of all of Earth's water. Second, of this 3.5%, only 1% is available for human use. Most fresh water is found in glaciers far from where anyone lives. Third, the amount of water that is useful for humans is being used faster than it can be cleaned and put back into the environment.

25   Now, knowing the facts about water, it is our job to make sure we use Earth's water wisely.

Time

Word Count 350 words

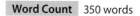

Circle the right answer.

1. This reading is about
   a. why Earth is different colors.
   b. the amount and types of Earth's water.
   c. who uses the most water on Earth.

2. Why is Earth also called the Blue Planet?
   a. It looks blue due to all of the water.
   b. It is a special planet because of water.
   c. It is surrounded by blue sky.

3. The writer says for consistency Earth is covered by
   a. 71% water.
   b. 3.5% water.
   c. 1% water.

4. Which of the following is NOT mentioned as a source of fresh water?
   a. Glaciers
   b. Oceans
   c. Water in the ground

5. The writer says that water is part of a closed system, meaning
   a. the amount of water becomes less and less.
   b. water is not lost.
   c. water is hard to find.

Score _____

Extra Practice

Write the right word in each blank to complete the summary.

concerned	solid	wisely	amount	liquid

Earth is special because the 1. _____ of water on its surface is more than that of any other planet. Most of Earth's water is salt water, and it is found in 2. _____ form. Only 3.5% of water on Earth is fresh water, and most of that is trapped in glaciers in 3. _____ form. Many people are 4. _____ that there is not enough water available for everyone to use. Therefore, it is important to use water 5. _____ .

Glaciers

Glaciers cover about 10% of the land on Earth, and they hold about 75% of Earth's fresh water. Glaciers are large pieces of tightly packed ice and snow. Glaciers only form where it is very cold. Every year, new snow falls on top of the old snow, and it is not warm enough for the snow to melt. The layers of snow press down on each other, and as they

5 press down on each other, the snow crystals start to change. They get smaller, and air pockets are pushed out of the snow. This allows the crystals to grow longer. This is the step between when snow is packed tightly together and when it becomes ice. Over time, the snow layer at the bottom of all the other snow layers becomes ice. The whole process of making a glacier takes about 100 years.

10 The ice inside a glacier gets packed more tightly every year, and this has a big effect on the ice crystals. Some ice is packed so tightly that it looks like it is blue. This is because there is a difference between the snow on top of a glacier and the ice of the glacier. The snow on top looks white because it reflects all of the light. But the ice layers of the glacier do not have many air pockets. They take in different parts of light, but they reflect blue

15 light.

Some of the glaciers on Earth may be very old. In fact, scientists think that a few glaciers have ice that is about 8 million years old. Not all of the glaciers are this old, though. A number of glaciers in Alaska are only about 100 years old.

There are different types of glaciers, and they form in various places. They are

20 affected by the weather and environment around them. For example, ice caps are like blankets of snow and ice. An ice stream is a kind of glacier that forms on another glacier, and it looks like a frozen river. Rock glaciers are made when ice, rock, and other objects get mixed

25 together.

Word Count 350 words

Time _____

Circle the right answer.

1. This reading is about
   a. different types of snow in Alaska.
   b. the forming of glaciers.
   c. how light is changed by ice.

2. Glaciers are made by
   a. layers of snow building up on top of each other.
   b. rocks and other objects that form layers.
   c. light passing through ice crystals.

3. Which of the following is NOT mentioned about glaciers?
   a. About 75% of Earth's fresh water is in glaciers.
   b. Glaciers cover about 10% of the land on Earth.
   c. All glaciers are about 8 million years old.

4. The writer talks about Alaska's glaciers because
   a. they are the oldest glaciers on Earth.
   b. some of them are not very old.
   c. the rocks found inside of them are valuable.

5. The ice on glaciers reflects blue light because
   a. there are no air pockets.
   b. it is millions of years old.
   c. snow reflects white light.

 Score _____

Extra Practice

Choose the word or phrase with a similar meaning as the underlined part.

1. The <u>ice caps</u> on many mountains grow smaller year by year.   snow / rocks

2. The <u>process</u> to form a glacier takes about 100 years.   effect / steps

3. As snow is <u>packed</u> more tightly, it begins to turn to ice.   pressed / mixed

4. As the salt water dried, <u>small blocks</u> of salt formed.   blankets / crystals

5. The glaciers found on each continent take <u>various</u> forms.   different / similar

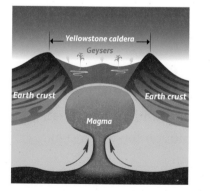

The Yellowstone Caldera

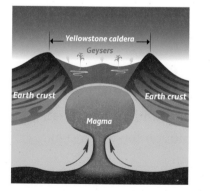
In the state of Wyoming, in the western part of the US, can be found Yellowstone National Park. It is a place of wild animals and natural wonders. It also contains a volcano in an area known as the Yellowstone Caldera.

A caldera is like a big bowl at the top of a volcano. It is formed when hot, liquid rock
5   is forced out of a volcano in a huge eruption. Scientists say that Yellowstone has seen three of these big eruptions over the past two million years. They believe the last one occurred more than 600 thousand years ago. Scientists also believe the material forced out of the volcano was equal to about half the size of Mt. Everest! The caldera left by that eruption is one of the largest in the world. It is 72 km long and 55 km wide.

10 Since that eruption long ago, life on the caldera has returned to normal. Wild animals are everywhere in the forests. Until the 1800s, the place was known only to local people. In 1872, the Yellowstone Caldera became the first national park in the US. But it was not because of the animals and forests. The caldera was an amazing natural wonder because of what came up from it.

15 In Yellowstone Park, there is a large area of rising steam and pools of hot water. The water in some of the pools is hot enough to cook food. Sometimes, a jet of water called a geyser will suddenly shoot into the air. These natural wonders draw people to the park. They are caused by the hot, liquid rock that lies deep within the caldera. But many park visitors probably don't realize that they are really inside a volcano. And the volcano is not dead;
20 it is only sleeping. It could erupt again at any time. In fact, recently there has been some movement of the ground in Yellowstone. It has been pushed up! Some scientists think that means another huge eruption may happen again. If the sleeping giant under Yellowstone ever wakes up again, the whole world will know.

Word Count 350 words

Circle the right answer.

1. This reading is about
   a. a visit to Yellowstone National Park.
   b. the animals of Yellowstone National Park.
   c. the Yellowstone National Park volcano.

2. Which of these is NOT true about the Yellowstone Caldera?
   a. It's the top of a sleeping volcano.
   b. There is no danger of an eruption.
   c. It is very large.

3. The writer says that a caldera is formed
   a. from a volcanic eruption.
   b. by steam.
   c. inside geysers.

4. The material blown off the Yellowstone volcano in the last eruption was
   a. similar in amount to the size of a mountain.
   b. made of jets of water combined with liquid rock.
   c. not as much as that of many active volcanoes studied today.

5. Scientists think there could be another eruption of the Yellowstone Caldera because
   a. the water in the pools is getting hotter.
   b. the ground in the park is rising.
   c. there are more geysers than before.

 Score _____

Extra Practice

Write the right word in each blank to complete the summary.

wonder	jets	caldera	liquid	erupted

   The 1. _____ in Yellowstone National Park is one of the biggest in the world. It was formed when a volcano 2. _____ several thousand years ago. The volcano is now sleeping, but hot, 3. _____ rock is still deep inside. This is what causes geysers to shoot 4. _____ of steam into the air. Though the volcano may awake again, this does not stop people from visiting this natural 5. _____.

The Ring of Fire

In 1521, Ferdinand Magellan sailed from Portugal around what is now South America. He found a body of water that was very peaceful and had good winds. He named this the "Mar Pacifico," which means the "Peaceful Sea." The Pacific Ocean might have been peaceful for Magellan, but the
5   land around it can be very active. That land has come to be known as "the Ring of Fire."

The Ring of Fire is 40,000 km long. It runs along the land that lies all around the Pacific Ocean. Most of the world's largest volcanic eruptions and largest earthquakes have happened around the ring. The ring runs all the way along the western side of South and North America up to Alaska. It then goes down the eastern side of Asia, down to New
10   Zealand, and then to Antarctica.

What causes so many eruptions and earthquakes around the Ring of Fire? The answer is the movement of tectonic plates. Tectonic plates are large sections that form the surface of the Earth. Those plates are always moving. The tectonic plates under the Pacific Ocean are moving in a way that the heavier tectonic plates move under lighter plates. The
15   heavy plates are under the sea, and the light plates are the land people live on. The heavier plates are forced down into the hot part of the Earth. There the plate material melts and in time may come out from under the earth as hot, liquid rock. This liquid rock is what causes volcanoes to erupt. The Ring of Fire gets its name from the volcanoes caused by this process.

20   There are more than 450 volcanoes along the Ring of Fire. Some of them are not active, but many are and could erupt at any time. But volcanoes are not the greatest danger; earthquakes are. The largest earthquake ever measured hit Chile in 1960. That earthquake killed thousands of people in Chile, and the ocean wave it caused killed more people 10,000 km away in Hawaii.

25   As long as the tectonic plates under the Pacific Ocean keep moving, the Ring of Fire will remain active.

Time

Word Count 350 words

Comprehension Questions

Circle the right answer.

1. This reading is about
   a. Magellan's great discovery.
   b. an area of volcanoes and earthquakes.
   c. a dangerous circle of fire.

2. The Ring of Fire is found in the land
   a. around the Atlantic Ocean.
   b. around the Pacific Ocean.
   c. around South America.

3. Volcanoes in the Ring of Fire are caused by
   a. movement of tectonic plates.
   b. earthquakes.
   c. waves in the Pacific Ocean.

4. Which of the following is NOT true of the ring?
   a. It is 40,000 km long.
   b. The largest earthquakes and volcanic eruptions happened there.
   c. There are more than 1,000 volcanoes in it.

5. The 1960 Chile earthquake
   a. was the largest earthquake ever measured.
   b. killed millions of people in Chile.
   c. caused people to die in New Zealand.

 Score _____

Extra Practice

Choose the word or phrase with a similar meaning as the underlined part.

1. The Ring of Fire contains many <u>active</u> volcanoes.   sleeping / erupting

2. Big volcanic <u>eruptions</u> are scary, but they usually do not happen often.   explosions / plates

3. When tectonic <u>plates</u> hit each other, there are earthquakes.   blocks / forces

4. Many people are <u>forced</u> to leave their homes during natural disasters.   melted / made

5. The <u>shaking land</u> caused some buildings to fall.   earthquake / storm

Chapter 4 History

A Match the picture with the right word.

1. _____

2. _____

3. _____

4. _____

a. cannon

b. kingdoms

c. terracotta

d. claim

e. emperor

f. weapons

g. clay bricks

h. tomb

5. _____

6. _____

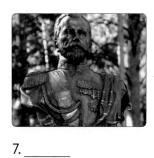

7. _____

8. _____

B **Choose the right word.**

1. You can _____ a kilometer (1,000 meters) to be a little more than half a mile.
   a. estimate   b. offer   c. produce
2. The Terracotta Army is an army of clay men believed to ___ the tomb of a Chinese emperor.
   a. claim   b. demand   c. protect
3. Two students saw the dollar on the floor, but ___ of them claimed it as their own.
   a. all   b. neither   c. some
4. Important weapons used to protect the kingdom during the war were guns and ___.
   a. cannons   b. centuries   c. princes
5. Slaves were ordered by the governor to make more ___ for building roads in the city.
   a. bricks   b. castles   c. towers

C **Answer these questions. Then ask your classmates. Are your answers similar?**

Classmate's Answers

1. The best way to learn about history is by _____.   _____
2. A world leader I know about is _____.   _____
3. If I could live during any time in the past, it would be _____. _____
4. Someone from the past I would like to meet is _____.   _____

D **Look at each group of words. Circle the one that does not belong. Why doesn't it belong?**

1. terracotta   brick   water   clay
2. dollar   kilometer   meter   mile
3. capture   claim   estimate   take
4. emperor   governor   king   researcher
5. weapon   tomb   knife   cannon

Proper Nouns to Know

Study these words that you will find in the readings for this chapter.

Babylon	Baghdad, Iraq	British	California	China
England	Europe	Germany	Hammurabi	
Jewish Bible	London	Malbork Castle	Mesopotamia	
Nebuchadnezzar	Poland	Qin Shi Huang	Russia/Russians	
Shaanxi Province	Sima Qian	Washington	William the Conqueror	

Castles in Europe

The first castles were built in Europe around the 9th century. These castles were different from the kinds of buildings that were made before them. These castles were very strong buildings where a king or prince could live safely with his army around
5   him. Such castles let the king or prince watch out for attacks and keep out the people he did not like. The castles also let the king or prince watch the people who lived around the castle.

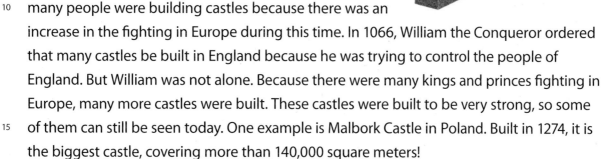

There were not many castles in Europe around 900 AD, but around 1000 AD things changed. Suddenly,
10   many people were building castles because there was an increase in the fighting in Europe during this time. In 1066, William the Conqueror ordered that many castles be built in England because he was trying to control the people of England. But William was not alone. Because there were many kings and princes fighting in Europe, many more castles were built. These castles were built to be very strong, so some
15   of them can still be seen today. One example is Malbork Castle in Poland. Built in 1274, it is the biggest castle, covering more than 140,000 square meters!

The first castles used a simple design. A tower was put on top of a lot of earth. All this earth was put under the tower to make it very tall. Moving all this earth made a huge hole all around the tower. Often, this large hole was filled with water. Stone or wood bridges
20   were used to go across this water to get into the tower. A wall was built around the open area near the tower. The family of the king or prince and some of the people who served him lived within this area so that they would be safe. The first castles were made largely of wood, but stone became more popular over time. This was because wood catches fire and burns easily. Stone was a better choice for castles. However, when attackers started to use
25   cannons, even the stone walls could not protect the people in the castle.

Word Count   350 words

Time

Comprehension Questions

Circle the right answer.

1. This reading is about

    a. how a king built castles in England and Poland.

    b. why people started building castles in Europe.

    c. a history of how kings and princes fought in Europe.

2. The writer says that castles were built to

    a. protect against fire by using stone.

    b. fight against the kings of England and Poland.

    c. watch people and protect against attack.

3. Which of the following is NOT true?

    a. People did not build castles before 1274.

    b. An old castle can still be seen today in Poland.

    c. William the Conqueror built castles in England.

4. Malbork Castle is mentioned by the writer because

    a. it is a strong castle that you can see today.

    b. it was built by William the Conqueror.

    c. it was created from wood and stone to stand against cannons.

5. What did the first castles have in common?

    a. They were built from stone and had a set of towers.

    b. They had a simple design and were made largely from wood.

    c. They kept attackers out and used cannons to protect people.

 Score _____

Extra Practice

Write the right word in each blank to complete the summary.

century	tower	increased	cannons	attacks

    Castles were first built in Europe in the 9th 1. _____. However, the number of castles quickly 2. _____ when fighting in Europe also increased. Many castles were surrounded by water and had a tall 3. _____. Stone was a popular choice for building the castles, but with the invention of 4. _____, even stone could not protect the people inside from 5. _____. In any case, most castles were built to be strong, so there are many still standing in Europe today.

The Pig War

The year was 1859. America and England had already fought two wars. Now, they were at peace. But one day a pig got hungry. And it nearly caused another war between the two countries.

The pig was owned by a British man who lived on a small island. The island was just 5 off of the western part of North America. Both England and the US said the island was theirs. Across the island from the British man lived some American farmers. Everyone on the island got along peacefully. But the peace ended the day the British man's pig decided to eat some of an American farmer's potatoes.

One of the American farmers shot and killed the pig. Then the pig's owner 10 demanded $100 from the man who shot the animal. That was a lot of money, so the farmer refused to pay it. The British and Americans began to argue, and the situation got worse. The farmers asked the governor over the island at that time for help. He sent a group of soldiers to protect the farmers. The British answered by sending 2,000 soldiers. The British were on one side of the island, and the Americans were on the other. The problem that 15 began with the pig was about to become a shooting war.

When news of the problem reached Washington and London, both leaders were surprised. Neither country wanted another war. They sent some men to try to fix the problem. After a discussion, it was decided that each country would keep a small group of soldiers on the island. They would stay there until the two countries could decide who 20 owned the island. Then the others would have to leave.

Twelve years went by. Neither side wanted to give up the island, but they knew they had to do something. They asked the leader of Germany to help decide. After nearly a year of discussion, a decision was made. America would get the island.

25 Finally, the Pig War was over, and only one shot had been fired. That was the shot that killed the pig!

 Time _____

Word Count 350 words

Circle the right answer.

1. This reading is about
   a. which country owned an island.
   b. a war between pigs.
   c. a war fought using farm animals.

2. The problem on the island started when
   a. an American shot a British man.
   b. a group of soldiers came to the island.
   c. a farmer killed a pig.

3. Which of these is NOT true according to the reading?
   a. America and Britain both said the island was theirs.
   b. In the end, Britain got the island.
   c. Neither country wanted to fight another war.

4. The two countries kept soldiers on the island
   a. one year.
   b. five years.
   c. twelve years.

5. When Britain and America could not solve the problem, they turned to
   a. the French.
   b. the Germans.
   c. New Zealand.

 Score _____

Extra Practice

Choose the word or phrase with a similar meaning as the underlined part.

1. People can <u>argue</u> for silly reasons.   disagree / shoot

2. <u>Wars</u> are expensive and kill many people.   Decisions / Fights

3. When both sides <u>refuse</u> to give up, the situation becomes worse.   discuss / don't want

4. A person is not always given what he <u>demands.</u>   asks for / reaches

5. The <u>person with power</u> made the final decision.   peace / leader

A Great Deal for the US

By the middle of the 1800s, Russia had given up trying to develop the land they claimed along the northwest Pacific area of North America. In 1867, they sold the land to the United States. It was to be one of the most important deals in American history.

The land that Russia sold became the US state of Alaska. Alaska is huge, about one

5 tenth the size of Russia, and the US paid only $7.2 million for it. Russia sold it because they thought that the US was going to take the land from them anyway. Also, Russia needed money at the time because it had just fought a war with England. They had offered Alaska to England and

10 the US, but England was not interested in buying it. That was a lucky break for the United States.

The sale helped the US rise as a power in the Asia-Pacific area. Up to that time, US land reached only as far west as California. Now, the land that was part of the US came within 100

15 kilometers of Russia. On top of that, Alaska had lots of natural riches!

Before Russia sold Alaska, the land was known as a mostly frozen desert with a lot of animals. Some brave explorers made money selling the skins of those animals, but the money was theirs. It did not do Russia any good. After the US bought Alaska, the land became much more valuable. In 1896, gold was discovered there. Suddenly, Alaska was

20 worth much more than $7 million. Alaska still produces a lot of gold. Though nobody knows the value of all the gold that Alaska has produced, it is estimated that more than 2.5 million pounds of gold has been taken from the ground there.

And Alaska has other things that make it valuable. Besides gold digging, fishing is an important business, earning hundreds of millions of dollars each year. Also, Alaska has a lot

25 of oil in the ground. Selling Alaska was a very bad deal for the Russians, but buying it was one of the best deals the US ever made.

Word Count 350 words

Time

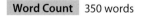

Comprehension Questions

Circle the right answer.

1. This reading is about
   a. Russia buying Alaska.
   b. America buying Alaska.
   c. Britain selling Alaska.

2. What did Russia think would happen to Alaska?
   a. It would become valuable.
   b. England would use it for a war.
   c. The US would take it.

3. Which of these is NOT true about Alaska?
   a. Russia bought it from England.
   b. It is mostly a frozen desert.
   c. It is very valuable land.

4. How did buying Alaska help the US rise to power?
   a. The US could build more ships.
   b. The US could sell things to England.
   c. The US had more land in the west.

5. What suddenly made Alaska a very valuable place?
   a. Trees
   b. Gold
   c. Animal skins

Score _____

Extra Practice

Write the right word in each blank to complete the summary.

deal	dollars	discovered	valuable	produce

The US bought Alaska from Russia for just seven million 1. _____. Alaska is very 2. _____ to the US because there are many natural resources there. For example, gold was 3. _____ there in 1896. In addition, resources like oil and even fish from Alaska 4. _____ a lot of money today. Buying Alaska was a very good 5. _____ for the US.

The Terracotta Army

In 1974, in the Shaanxi Province in China, some farmers were digging a hole for a well. They were looking for water, but they found something amazing. They found an army. It was an army made of clay.

After more digging, people found a huge number of terracotta
5   figures buried there. Terracotta is a type of baked clay, so the figures came to be known as the Terracotta Army. The army has 8,000 men and 670 horses in it. Qin Shi Huang ordered this army to be made to protect himself in the next life after his death. Along with the soldiers to protect him, there were other terracotta figures. Some of them were musicians and important people who
10   worked for the emperor.

In 246 BC, Qin Shi Huang became the first Emperor of China. He was only thirteen years old when he became emperor. Right away, work began on his burial ground. We know of the story of the emperor and his tomb from the Chinese writer Sima Qian. Sima lived about a hundred years after Qin Shi Huang. He says that 700,000 men worked on
15   the army of statues, which took forty years to complete. Given the size of the tomb, that number is probably correct. The total area of the burial site is almost a hundred square kilometers!

The soldiers in the Terracotta Army were just models, but their weapons were not. They each had some of the finest weapons of their time. Chinese metal workers must have been
20   very skilled and smart. The knives and other weapons they made are all still very sharp. Also, some of the weapons were covered with special chemicals that protected them.

As amazing as the Terracotta Army is, it may not be the high point of the emperor's tomb. Still unopened is the part where his body was buried, and this part of the tomb is huge. It is as big as a football field! Researchers are waiting to open it. They want to be sure
25   they can protect what's inside. If it's anything like the clay figures, it is sure to be amazing.

Word Count 350 words

Time _____

Comprehension Questions

Circle the right answer.

1. This reading is about
   a. a historical treasure that was found.
   b. how an emperor made his army stronger.
   c. a war between farmers and soldiers.

2. Which of these is NOT true according to the article?
   a. There were 8,000 clay soldiers.
   b. The tomb is still unopened.
   c. The soldiers had weapons of gold.

3. Qin Shi Huang's army was buried with him
   a. because he was very young.
   b. to protect him.
   c. a hundred years after he died.

4. The weapons found in the tomb were
   a. very well made.
   b. poorly made.
   c. made of wood.

5. Qin Shi Huang's tomb is unusual because
   a. it is made of metal.
   b. it shaped like a ball.
   c. it is very big.

Score _____

Extra Practice

Choose the word or phrase with a similar meaning as the underlined part.

1. Clay is a good material for making statues and pots.   Metal / Earth

2. Emperors held a lot of power over their people.   Kings / Musicians

3. Many people choose to be put in the ground after they die.   buried / burned

4. Some burial sites are underground; others are in caves.   figures / tombs

5. Weapons are often used in war to protect people.   Guns / Chemicals

The Brick Kingdom

Thousands of years ago, stone was used to build many of the great cities. But in Mesopotamia, there was no stone for building. Yet, one of the greatest kingdoms of the old world would be built there, and it would be built of brick.

5   According to the Jewish Bible, the first people in southern Mesopotamia wanted to build a tower all the way to the sky. They wanted to be famous throughout the world. The Bible says that they "burned bricks in the fire." Baked bricks, of course, are almost as hard as stone, so the early Mesopotamians could build high buildings. Those early brick makers never built their tower to the sky, but they would go on to build cities of bricks. One of the cities they built became the ancient kingdom of Babylon.

10   Babylon, researchers say, was probably the largest city in the world in its day with a population of more than 200,000. In the 18th century BC, Hammurabi was king of Babylon. He is very famous, of course, for the laws he made. After the death of Hammurabi, Babylon also began to die. The city was finally torn down by the Assyrians. But that was not the end of Babylon.

15   In the 7th century BC, King Nebuchadnezzar began a project to build the city again. Once again, Babylon was built from brick. From ancient texts, we learn that Nebuchadnezzar built huge buildings. In fact, Babylon became famous for its giant buildings, one of which was more than ninety meters high. Perhaps Nebuchadnezzar was trying to be famous like those people in the Bible. But he did do one thing to make sure 20 people remembered his name. He had his name stamped on every brick that was used to build Babylon's broken walls again. Nebuchadnezzar's kingdom did not last long, though. First, the Persians moved in, and then the Greeks. Finally, the desert sand covered Babylon.

    Just south of Baghdad, Iraq, is what's left of the 25 kingdom of Babylon. It is now just a lot of bricks, but they bring to memory a great kingdom from long ago.

Time _____

Word Count   350 words

Comprehension Questions

Circle the right answer.

1. This reading is about
   a. the building of Babylon.
   b. how to make bricks.
   c. a king who loved bricks.

2. According to the Bible, the first people in southern Mesopotamia wanted to
   a. become rich.
   b. become famous.
   c. become brick makers.

3. Babylon was built of brick because
   a. there was no stone.
   b. bricks were cheap.
   c. the people didn't plan to live there long.

4. Which of the following is NOT true according to the article?
   a. Hammurabi was king of Babylon.
   b. Nebuchadnezzar's kingdom did not last a long time.
   c. Babylon is part of Greece now.

5. To make sure his name would be remembered, Nebuchadnezzar
   a. wrote his name on Babylon's largest building.
   b. had his name written on each brick.
   c. wrote a book about himself.

 Score _____

Extra Practice

Write the right word in each blank to complete the summary.

memory	kingdom	brick	population	death

Babylon was a great 1. _____. The city's buildings were made of bricks, and it was one of the biggest cities of that time with a 2. _____ of 200,000 people. King Hammurabi once ruled Babylon, but after his 3. _____, the kingdom fell. Later, another king, Nebuchadnezzar rebuilt the 4. _____ kingdom again. This later kingdom did not last long either. Other people took over the city, and little is now left but the 5. _____ of what had been.

Chapter 5 Economics

A Which of the following are associated with banks or money? Circle six words or phrases.

account

concept

crowdfund

encourage

fee

loan

reason

minimum wage

tax

universal

B Match the parts to make correct sentences.

1. When you need money, you •   • a fallacy because someone •   • employers will not.

2. The concept of "free" is •   • can get a loan from a bank •   • for a good or service.

3. A monopoly is bad since •   • one doesn't pay much to see doctors, •   • must always pay.

4. Under universal healthcare, •   • customers have no choice •   • or crowdfund online.

5. If the minimum wage goes up, •   • employees will be happy; •   • but taxes are high.

C Work in groups with your classmates. Can you think of examples for all of these ideas related to economics? Share your examples with the class.

Reasons why someone might borrow money:	Services for which many people pay fees:	Jobs that pay minimum wage:	An important concept in economics:

 D Fill in the blanks with words from the box to make common phrases.

account	balance	crowdfund	employee	fallacy
loan	market	quality	taxes	universal

1. improve product _____

2. monopolize the _____

3. _____ a project

4. believe an economic _____

5. hire a new _____

6. include all _____ and fees

7. open a bank _____

8. _____ healthcare

9. get a _____ for a car

10. _____ supply and demand

Proper Nouns to Know

Study these words that you will find in the readings for this chapter.

American	Domino's	France	Japan	Kickstarter

Mr. Pizza	Papa John's	Paypal	Pizza Hut

Supply and Demand

Supply and demand is an economic concept. Demand is how much of a thing or service people want to buy. Supply is how much is available to buy. The price of a thing or service is affected by the concept of supply and demand.

5　When many people want something, the demand for it goes up. However, if there is not enough of what they want to buy, the price goes up. The price of something can go very high. When this happens, most people cannot buy what they want, so the demand for the expensive thing

10　goes down. Businesses try to sell things or services to make money. They try to supply what people want. The best market situation is when supply and demand are in balance. This means that companies are making enough products that customers want to buy at a certain price.

Supply and demand are affected by many things. They can be affected by time and

15　what is going on in the world. For example, let's say a new phone comes out. The new phone is very special, so the company sets the price at $700. However, when the company sells the new phone is important. If the company sells its new phone right after a big holiday, many customers may not buy it. Demand will be low because people have already spent a lot of money buying food or gifts for the holiday. The company may have to lower the price to get

20　people to buy it. However, if the company sells the phone right before a holiday, it may do well. People may want to buy the phone as a present. They may also want to get a new phone for themselves. The demand for the phone then goes up. If the company does not have enough phones, it has to make some more. But that takes time. The phones that are available to people may then become more expensive. As the price goes up for the new phone, fewer

25　people will want to buy it. They will buy a less expensive phone or another present.

Word Count　350 words

Time _____

Comprehension Questions

Circle the right answer.

1. This reading is about
   a. how the demand for phones affects price.
   b. why the prices of certain services or things are high.
   c. how supply and demand works.

2. Supply is
   a. the amount of things or services provided by companies.
   b. the goods or services that people want to buy.
   c. the result of reaching the right price.

3. Which of the following is NOT mentioned as something that affects price?
   a. How many people really want to buy something
   b. How a business is named by the owners
   c. How much of a good or service is available

4. The writer mentions a new phone
   a. to explain why new phone prices are high.
   b. to talk about why people decide to buy phones.
   c. to show an economic concept.

5. The best market situation is when supply and demand are
   a. in balance.
   b. changing.
   c. controlled by the government.

 Score _____

Extra Practice

Choose the word or phrase with a similar meaning as the underlined part.

1. There is always a high <u>demand</u> for milk.   need / service

2. The <u>supply</u> of home phones is decreasing since most people   concept / amount
   use cell phones.

3. Big diamonds are expensive because not many <u>are available</u>.   exist / sell

4. New tech <u>products</u> are very popular.   situation / items

5. A company should try to <u>balance</u> supply and demand.   make even / buy

The Minimum Wage

The minimum wage is the lowest amount of money you are allowed to pay an employee to do a job. Some people, usually employees, think the minimum wage should be higher. Others, usually business owners, think the minimum wage should be lower.

An employee is poor when he or she works full-time and is only paid the minimum
5   wage. This is not enough money for one person to live on. It is also not enough money to take care of a family. Those working at minimum wage jobs need to find help to live. Poor workers usually get government help. They may get free food from food banks. Poor workers need to get government help to pay for hospital bills. Since these poor employees are working a lot, they do not have time to learn new skills. Some people say that business
10 owners who only pay the minimum wage are being unfair. They say these business owners benefit from having the government help out their poor workers. Some research shows that raising the minimum wage a little would not hurt businesses. But it would help many of the poor.

15 Some people think that the minimum wage is fine as it is. They say that no one should be working at a minimum wage job for a long time. Minimum wage jobs are only to bring in some income until the person can find a "real" job. Many business owners don't believe the research. They say
20 increasing the minimum wage would hurt them. If they need to pay workers more money, the business will not have enough money. Because the owners need to have money to stay in business, they will fire employees. Fewer people will have jobs. Businesses will not bring in new people. Business owners would also need to raise prices. They would need to get extra money to help pay the workers. Many business owners
25 say that if they raise prices, customers will not buy their products as often, or at all. The minimum wage is an issue that both employers and employees have strong opinions on!

Time

Word Count 350 words

Comprehension Questions

Circle the right answer.

1. This reading is about

    a. the ways that the minimum wage affects the government.

    b. how the minimum wage affects workers and business owners.

    c. why business owners should raise the minimum wage.

2. Which of the following is NOT mentioned as a problem for poor workers?

    a. They do not have time to learn new skills.

    b. They do not have enough money to live on.

    c. They have to pay a lot of tax on their wages.

3. Many poor workers need

    a. hospital help.

    b. government help.

    c. business help.

4. Business owners do not want to raise the minimum wage because

    a. they will have to raise prices.

    b. they will need government help.

    c. they will have to bring in more workers.

5. Business owners benefit from government help because

    a. they use government workers at the company.

    b. firing employees is a problem.

    c. their poor employees use it to live.

 Score _____

Extra Practice

Write the right word in each blank to complete the summary.

owners	benefit	wage	employees	products

The minimum 1. _____ is the lowest amount an employer can pay an employee per hour. Business 2. _____ usually want to keep the minimum wage low. They think if the amount they have to pay employees is more, then they will have to raise the price of their 3. _____ as well. However, 4. _____ think the minimum wage should be higher. Raising it would 5. _____ many who are poor.

How Monopolies Affect Economies

Monopoly is a popular board game that was first made in the 1930s. The goal of the game is to make other players pay you so that you become the richest player. Players must pay when they stop on something another player owns. Places on the board have colors, and when a player owns all of a color, he or she can make a lot more money. If you have played this board game, you already have a good idea of what the word "monopoly" means.

A monopoly is a situation in which a business or a company controls the whole market to provide a certain good or service. Monopolies can be bad. Why is that? For one thing, when a business has a monopoly, there is no more competition. This means that the business can set its own prices as high as it wants. After all, there is no one to provide the same or similar good or service at a lower price. A business with a monopoly may also offer lower quality products or services. And in addition, a business with a monopoly has no need to improve its products or services.

Take pizza for example. Luckily, there is no pizza company that has a monopoly over pizza. In fact, there are many choices of pizza restaurants. Some examples are Pizza Hut, Papa John's, Domino's, and Mr. Pizza. Because there are so many different pizza restaurants, there is a lot of competition among the pizza companies to attract customers. If the pizza costs too much, customers will go to a cheaper pizza restaurant. If the pizza tastes bad, the customers will go somewhere else. Now imagine if there were only one pizza company. If this were the case, a company with a monopoly over pizza could make the price of pizza very high. It could also make bad-tasting pizza, but customers would have no other place to get better-tasting pizza.

In short, monopolies are bad for the economy and for customers. It takes the power of buying away from the customer and puts it in the hands of the company.

Time _____

Word Count 350 words

Comprehension Questions

Circle the right answer.

1. This reading is about
   a. how to play Monopoly.
   b. the negative side of monopolies.
   c. how to build a monopoly.

2. A monopoly occurs when a business
   a. makes a new service or product.
   b. is the only one to provide a service or product.
   c. can no longer offer a service or product.

3. When a business with a monopoly no longer has any competition, it
   a. can set higher prices.
   b. will make better products.
   c. has to offer cheaper prices.

4. The writer says that a business with a monopoly does not need to
   a. advertise its services or products.
   b. rent houses and hotels.
   c. research ways to improve its services or products.

5. The writer thinks that monopolies are bad because they take away
   a. the ability of customers to choose.
   b. people's money.
   c. the buying power of the dollar.

 Score _____

Extra Practice

Choose the word or phrase with a similar meaning as the underlined part.

1. A company with <u>a monopoly</u> is bad for the market.   full control / good quality

2. <u>Customers</u> like to have a choice of products.   Buyers / Competition

3. Competition makes <u>products</u> better.   situations / items

4. The <u>quality</u> of service is important to customers.   level / goal

5. Cheaper prices will <u>attract</u> more customers.   taste / interest

The Job of Banks

Banks are businesses where people can put their money to keep it safe until it is needed. Banks also pay interest on money kept in the bank. This is a percentage of money that is given to a person based on how much he or she has in the bank. Banks also offer loans. In other words, banks allow people to borrow money. Loans are usually used for paying for expensive things such as a house or a car, or paying for college. The person must then pay interest on the loan. This is a percentage that is added on top of the borrowed money that must be paid back to the bank. The interest that is collected is how banks make money. People with money in bank accounts can use their accounts to pay bills either with checks or using online pay services offered through a bank's website.

These days, there are other ways to do banking. First, some countries such as France and Japan have combined post office services and simple banking services. This means that a person can put in or take out money at a post office. There are also internet companies such as Kickstarter that allow people to crowdfund new business ideas. In other words, instead of going to the bank for money, people can now raise money from a large group of people who are willing to give money in support of a business idea. Some think that this method of borrowing money could even spread to borrowing money for reasons other than business as well. In addition, there are other internet services, such as Paypal, that can provide some of the banking needs of customers.

If there are other ways to do what banks are set up to do—put in and take out money, borrow money, and pay bills—are banks necessary? Some people will argue that banks are no longer necessary if we are able to use a combination of other ways of banking. They believe that people could, in fact, save more money if a bank is not used as a middle man.

Word Count 350 words

Time

Comprehension Questions

Circle the right answer.

1. This reading is about
   a. the purpose and need of banks.
   b. different types of banks.
   c. how to get a loan.

2. Which of the following is NOT mentioned as a reason for using a bank?
   a. To keep money safe
   b. To pay for college
   c. To help with getting a job

3. The writer says some countries like Japan and France offer simple banking services at
   a. the supermarket.
   b. the police station.
   c. the post office.

4. Kickstarter is another way to raise money by
   a. getting money from people directly.
   b. going to many different banks.
   c. going to another country.

5. The writer thinks banks
   a. might become more like Kickstarter.
   b. may not be around forever.
   c. will stay for a long time.

Score _____

Extra Practice

Write the right word in each blank to complete the summary.

amount	argue	account	combined	loans

Banks allow people to keep money safe in a(n) 1. _____. They also provide 2. _____ so that people can pay for things like a house, car, or college. Some people 3. _____ that banks are not necessary these days. In some countries, post offices have 4. _____ postal and banking services. In addition, people can crowdfund if they need to borrow a large 5. _____ of money. Banks may not be around forever.

The Economic Fallacy of Free

If something is free, it will attract many people. Whether it's a free meal, a free trip, or a free visit to the zoo, most people would take it. After all, who doesn't like getting something for free? If it is free, it doesn't cost anything. Right? Wrong. This is a mistaken idea, or economic fallacy.

5   There is a popular saying that states, "There is no such thing as a free lunch." The saying came from a common practice in some American restaurants. A restaurant might give a free meal to anyone who bought at least one drink as a way to encourage people to come to the restaurant. Even though the meal was free, most people would end up buying more than one drink. This simple example shows how it is not possible to get anything

10 without paying a cost. In this case, the cost of the meal is included in the price of the drinks.

Think about a national park with no fee to enter. A park visit is not actually free. Though there is no fee to enter, there is always a cost. People have paid for the building of the park and keeping the park clean by their taxes. Some countries in Europe offer

15 universal or free medical care for all of their people. However, this "free" medical care is not actually free. Though one may not pay anything to visit the doctor's office, doctors still need to be paid. Hospitals also need money to pay for employees, cleaning, and supplies. Where does the money come from? Taxes. Many of these countries have a tax rate above 40% to pay for such services. In comparison, for countries such as the US, where people

20 pay for health services, the tax rate is much lower, at 10-30%.

Sometimes, a city or business may hold events such as a free movie or a free concert in the park. These, too, are not actually free. Though the people attending may not pay for a ticket to enjoy these events, someone is paying in their place.

25 Everything has a price. Nothing is free.

Word Count   350 words

Time

Comprehension Questions

Circle the right answer.

1. This reading is about
   a. the mistaken belief that things can be free.
   b. laws that governments make to control the economy.
   c. how to get more things for free.

2. The writer says that the saying, "There is no such thing as a free lunch," came from a practice in American
   a. schools.
   b. restaurants.
   c. hospitals.

3. Universal healthcare is offered in many countries in
   a. South America.
   b. Asia.
   c. Europe.

4. Which is NOT mentioned as an example of something that is free?
   a. A concert in the park
   b. Healthcare
   c. Housing

5. The writer says that nothing is
   a. free.
   b. universal.
   c. taxed.

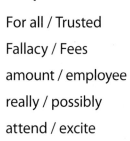 Score _____

Extra Practice

Choose the word or phrase with a similar meaning as the underlined part.

1. <u>Universal</u> healthcare is not offered in the US. — For all / Trusted

2. <u>Taxes</u> are used to help maintain national and public parks. — Fallacy / Fees

3. The tax <u>rate</u> is higher in countries that offer more free public services. — amount / employee

4. Almost all things are not <u>actually</u> free. — really / possibly

5. Groceries offer free samples to <u>encourage</u> people to buy products. — attend / excite

Chapter 6 Literature

A Look at the pictures. Write the right words.

advertisement	copyright	journals	market
political	profits	publish	religious

In the book industry:

1. declining _____

2. _____ online

3. _____ research

4. in-store _____

Things that are written:

5. _____ page

6. _____ books

7. _____ cartoons

8. scientific _____

B Write the right word in each blank.

ban	copyright	freedom	poet
political	protection	publish	weird

1. When writing poetry, a _____ may use grammar that seems _____ in order to make the ends of certain lines rhyme.

2. Governments in some countries _____ foreign books because those books discuss a _____ position the government doesn't like.

3. There is religious _____ in Europe and the Americas to write and _____ books about any of the world's religions.

4. Writers' works have _____ under international _____ laws.

C Work with a classmate. Think about authors and literature. Write two …

1. … books that made huge profits for the publisher.   _____ and _____

2. … industries that are related to making books.   _____ and _____

3. … famous journals of science or research.   _____ and _____

4. … reasons bookstore business has declined.   _____ and _____

D Read about each writer. Then write the right name in each blank.

Einstein	Homer	Shakespeare	Twain

around 700 BC poems *The Odyssey*	late 1500s plays and poems *Hamlet*	late 1800s books *Tom Sawyer*	early 1900s books and journal articles *Relativity*

1. _____   2. _____   3. _____   4. _____

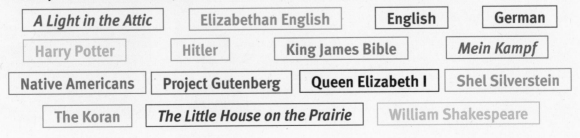

Proper Nouns to Know

Study these words that you will find in the readings for this chapter.

A Light in the Attic	Elizabethan English	**English**	German

| Harry Potter | Hitler | King James Bible | *Mein Kampf* |

| Native Americans | Project Gutenberg | **Queen Elizabeth I** | Shel Silverstein |

| The Koran | *The Little House on the Prairie* | William Shakespeare |

Should Books Be Free to Read Online?

Have you ever needed to go to the library when it was closed? Or have you gone to the library and found that the book you really needed was not there? If that book were online, you would not

5 even need to leave the house to read it.

Some people and companies agree that books should be free online. The Project Gutenberg site has over 50,000 books on it, and you can read all of these books for free. Most of

10 these books are very old. But Project Gutenberg is not the only place to find free books. Google, for example, offers 20 million books or sections of books online. You can read only a few parts of some books, but there are other online books that you can read from start to finish for free. Free online books can be very useful. They can help you when you cannot go to the library. They can also help you perform

15 research on important topics. A number of books are too expensive to buy, so reading them online can save you money. Or if you want to buy a certain book, you can see what is inside of it before you get it.

While there are many good uses for online books, not everyone thinks they are a great idea. Some writers think that putting books online is bad for them. This is because

20 a writer gets paid for every copy of the book that is sold. If people can read books for free online, no one will buy writers' books and many writers will lose money. Since a lot of time goes into writing a book, many writers might stop writing because they cannot make a living. A group of writers also argued that Google was doing the wrong thing by putting books online for free. They said that Google was making a profit off of the writers' works.

25 This is because people will go look at Google to find the books they want to read. Google did not pay the writers for the use of their books.

Time

Word Count 350 words

Comprehension Questions

Circle the right answer.

1. This reading is about
   a. keeping books in the libraries.
   b. putting books on the internet.
   c. why Google created Project Gutenberg.

2. According to the reading, writers can lose money if
   a. people only read their books online for free.
   b. they use Google and Project Gutenberg for research.
   c. students can't find their books at the library.

3. Which of the following is NOT mentioned as a benefit of free online books?
   a. You can read expensive books for free.
   b. You can perform research on important topics.
   c. You can help writers out by reading their books.

4. Writers were arguing with Google because
   a. the company was not paying for their books.
   b. the company was buying too many books.
   c. the company was only paying some writers.

5. Online books can help people
   a. who want to sell their books to Google or Project Gutenberg.
   b. who cannot go to the library.
   c. who would like to join up with other writers.

 Score _____

Extra Practice

Write the right word in each blank to complete the summary.

profit	library	since	millions	online

In the past, books could only be found in a 1. _____ or bookstore, but now they are moving to the internet. In fact, Google already has 2. _____ of books online. Having books available 3. _____ can save a lot of time and money especially when doing research. However, writers are not happy about this 4. _____ people buy fewer books now. In addition, it seems unfair for Google to make a 5. _____ without paying anything back to writers.

The Decline of the Printed Word

Not long ago, reading the newspaper in the morning with a cup of coffee or in the evening after dinner was common. However, the newspaper industry has been declining over the past ten years. It's not only newspapers, though. Magazine companies are finding it hard to keep their readers. Buying physical books is also declining as well. Why is this
5 happening? Simply put, it's because of the internet.

It used to be that newspapers, magazines, and books were how people connected to the rest of the world and kept up with current events and interests. However, with 40% of the world connected to the internet, the need for the printed word is becoming much lower due to how easy it is to find information online. People no longer need to wait for a
10 newspaper or magazine to arrive. They can now find all the information or reading material they want on the internet whenever they want. No longer do people have to turn through large pages in the newspaper or carry magazines around. Anything and everything one might need can now easily be found through a computer or smartphone. Though books have faced a slower decline, the amount and use of e-books and e-readers have been on
15 the rise. After all, it is much easier to carry an e-book in one's back pocket or bag than it is to carry a heavy book around. E-books do not take up space in the home, and they are also always available when needed.

With fewer readers of printed newspapers and magazines, more advertisers are also moving to the internet and social media. As a result, a number of newspapers and
20 magazines have been forced out of business. Some others have even tried to move online in order to try and keep going.

If the current trend continues, the decline of the printed word may lead to a future generation that will not know what it is like to hold a newspaper, magazine, or book. To some, it will be a sign of the future. To
25 others, it will be the sad end of a valued tradition.

Word Count   350 words

Time _____

Circle the right answer.

1. This reading is about
   a. how newspapers and magazines make money.
   b. people reading less.
   c. what is happening to printed materials.

2. The writer says that the popularity of printed newspapers, magazines, and books
   a. is decreasing.
   b. is increasing.
   c. has stayed the same.

3. What does the writer say is causing people to lose interest in printed texts?
   a. People don't need to pay for books.
   b. People can get the information from somewhere else.
   c. People don't like all of the advertisements.

4. Which of the following is NOT mentioned as a benefit of online texts?
   a. Are easy to carry around
   b. Don't take up space
   c. Can be read in dark places

5. The writer says that a generation that does not know what it is to hold a newspaper is
   a. a sign of the future.
   b. the loss of a valued tradition.
   c. both a and b.

Score _____

Extra Practice

Choose the word or phrase with a similar meaning as the underlined part.

1. The newspaper <u>industry</u> is declining.   business / material
2. News and information can be found <u>on the internet</u>.   in magazines / online
3. Some people prefer e-books <u>due to</u> easy access.   therefore / because of
4. <u>Physical</u> books are being printed less.   Touchable / Valued
5. Many printing companies are being <u>forced</u> to shut down.   available / made

Copyright Laws

People can create things like buildings or computers. People can also create stories and songs. Since stories and songs are made up out of a person's mind and thoughts, they only exist on paper. This makes it easy for someone else to take a story or song away from the person who wrote it first. This is why the copyright is important. A copyright gives a
5   writer protection under the law for his or her work.

Every country has its own copyright laws. For example, US copyright laws say that any work that was published before 1923 is now public, and anyone can use it for free. Works that were written between 1923 and 1978 are protected for 95 years. Works that were written after 1978 are protected for the life of the writer
10   plus 70 years after that person dies. In Canada, the law is a little different. Works made in Canada are protected for the life of the writer plus 50 years. Copyrights were first started to encourage people to be creative. If people know their stories and songs will be safe, they can write many of them.

15   However, copyrights do more than just protect a writer's work. They also help companies that sell creative works like movies, books, or songs. Some of these companies are very large and own a lot of copyrights. Because they own so many, especially of older works, people cannot use stories or songs that are even 100 years old to create new things.
20   Research is another area where the copyright law is causing some trouble. Many scientists get money from governments to do research. This money comes from the people who live in that country. However, when scientists publish their research in certain science journals, people must pay to see it. Some of the science journals are very expensive. A number of scientists are not happy about this because it means that other researchers may not be
25   able to learn from their work. They are also unhappy because it means that the people who paid for their research now have to pay more to read the results.

Time _____

Word Count   350 words

Circle the right answer.

1. This reading is about
   a. why writers need to get a copyright for their work.
   b. how US and Canadian copyrights help large companies.
   c. what copyrights are for and some problems with them.

2. Some large companies own many copyrights so
   a. people cannot use stories or songs that are very old.
   b. people cannot make new stories or songs.
   c. people can only create things that the companies want.

3. Which of the following is NOT mentioned as a part of US copyright laws?
   a. Any work that was published before 1923 is free for the public to use.
   b. Works are protected for the life of the writer plus 50 years.
   c. Works that were written after 1978 are protected for the life of the writer plus 70 years.

4. Copyright laws can be a problem for scientists because
   a. other scientists may not be able to read the research.
   b. scientists will need to work for large companies to get paid.
   c. writers may not be able to make a living if they have to pay.

5. Copyright laws usually help people
   a. find a way to own more stories.
   b. protect their stories and songs.
   c. sell their research to journals.

Score _____

Extra Practice

Write the right word in each blank to complete the summary.

journals	protect	copyrights	research	encourages

1. _____ are important. They 2. _____ songs and stories so that they cannot be claimed by other people as their own. So, it 3. _____ people to be creative. People do not always agree with copyrights, though. For example, scientists do research and write for 4. _____, but people must pay for the journals to read the results. So, in the case of scientific 5. _____, copyrights can actually cause trouble.

Banned Books

Banned books are books that are not available because it is against the law to sell them or against the rules to have them. But who can ban books? And for what reason?

First, a country's government can ban a book. Sometimes, a government will ban a book because of a political reason. For example, *Mein Kampf*, the book that Hitler wrote
5   about himself, is banned in Germany because Hitler killed millions of people during his time as a German leader. A government might also ban a book because of religious reasons. Some countries have a state religion, meaning every person in the country should follow that certain religion. This means some religious books like the Bible or the Koran are banned in certain countries.

10   Second, schools and libraries can ban books. Usually when a school bans a book, it is because the teachers or parents do not want their children to read it. For example, the "Harry Potter" books are banned in some US and UK libraries because the story is too dark and the books seem to say good things about magic and witches. Another example is *The Little House on the Prairie*, a popular series of books about the time in America when
15   people were moving west away from cities into the wild, middle part of the country. These books were banned in some places because of the books' negative view toward Native Americans. Sometimes, the reason may seem silly such as the case of *A Light in the Attic*, a children's book by Shel Silverstein. This book was banned in some schools because the children in one story of the book break dishes so they won't have to
20   dry them. Parents thought that this and other similar types of stories in the book encouraged children not to respect their parents.

Banning a book can be seen as a way to protect the reader from harmful ideas. On the other hand, banning can be seen as taking away people's freedom. Whatever the reason may be, if the government
25   or enough adults don't want a book to be available, the book can be banned.

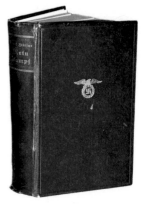

Time _____

Word Count 350 words

Comprehension Questions

Circle the right answer.

1. This reading is about
    a. good books to read.
    b. books people can't read.
    c. reasons for reading.

2. Which of the following is NOT mentioned as a group that can ban books?
    a. The government
    b. The police
    c. Schools

3. The writer says that the "Harry Potter" books are banned in some places because
    a. they describe life in the wild west.
    b. they say good things about magic and witches.
    c. they focus on the religion of the writer.

4. Books can be banned if enough people
    a. read them.
    b. don't like them.
    c. sell them.

5. The writer says that banning a book can
    a. protect readers from harmful ideas.
    b. give more freedom to people.
    c. save publishers money.

Score _____

Extra Practice

Choose the word or phrase with a similar meaning as the underlined part.

1. Banning a book can protect a child from <u>harmful</u> ideas.   unsafe / good

2. Countries with <u>state</u> religions may ban books from other religions.   national / free

3. Germany banned Hitler's book for <u>political</u> reasons.   library / government

4. Children in some stories do not <u>act the right way</u> toward adults.   seem silly / show respect

5. Some people think that banning books limits people's <u>freedom</u>.   independence / reasons

The Language of Shakespeare

Every student should read one of the plays by William Shakespeare. It will be a chance for those students to read some of the most amazing poetry ever written. But it will be hard. Shakespeare didn't use language like the rest of us.

William Shakespeare lived in the time of Queen Elizabeth I. The language spoken in
5 England at that time is known as Elizabethan English. The King James Bible was written in Elizabethan English, and it is still read by many people today. If people can understand the King James Bible, why is it so difficult to understand the plays of William Shakespeare?

One problem in understanding Shakespeare is the meaning of the words. Though about 95% of Shakespeare's words are still used in English today, a few of them now have
10 different meanings. One of the changes, for example, is the word "weird." To us, it means strange. In Shakespeare's day, it meant being able to see the future. Another example is "quick." It now means fast, but 400 years ago it meant alive.

While word meanings may be one problem, Shakespeare's order
15 of words is another problem. Typically, words are put together in a certain order in English. For example, we usually say, "John caught the ball." But Shakespeare was a poet, and, like all poets, he did not have to keep language rules. He would sometimes use the form, "John the ball caught." He did this to make the beats and sounds of each line of his poems
20 come out a certain way. But any high school student should easily be able to understand Shakespeare's creative word order. The problem, it seems, must be something else.

The biggest problem, perhaps, with understanding Shakespeare's plays is not so much Elizabethan English. It is understanding Shakespeare himself. He was, after all, a poet. Even great modern poets write things that readers might have trouble understanding. Students
25 will always have trouble understanding the language of Shakespeare. But if they don't give up, they will enjoy some of the greatest works ever written by the greatest of poets.

Time

Word Count 350 words

Comprehension Questions

Circle the right answer.

1. This reading is about

    a. how Shakespeare learned to speak English.

    b. how Shakespeare taught people his language.

    c. why people have trouble understanding Shakespeare.

2. According to the article, Shakespeare lived

    a. in the 1400s.

    b. in the Elizabethan Era.

    c. in Queen Elizabeth's castle.

3. Shakespeare's plays and the King James Bible are both written in

    a. Elizabethan English.

    b. common English.

    c. high English.

4. Which of the following is true according to the reading?

    a. Shakespeare created new meanings for many of the words in his plays.

    b. The English language is easier to learn today than it was in the past.

    c. Shakespeare changed normal word order to fit his poetry.

5. What is NOT mentioned as a reason why Shakespeare is hard to understand?

    a. Words in Elizabethan English had different meanings.

    b. Shakespeare had a different way of thinking.

    c. Shakespeare used language from the Bible.

 Score _____

Extra Practice

Write the right word in each blank to complete the summary.

weird	language	chance	certain	amazing

Shakespeare was a(n) 1. _____ poet and writer. However, many people today find it difficult to understand the 2. _____ of his plays and poems. One reason is because some words like "3. _____" or "quick" have a different meaning today than they did in Shakespeare's time. Another reason is because Shakespeare put words in a 4. _____ order that people are not used to. Even if it is hard, people should still give Shakespeare's writings a 5. _____!

Chapter 7

Space

A Check (✓) the right answer.

1. Which is longer?

☐ the wavelength of blue light

☐ one centimeter

2. Which is larger?

☐ a toy rocket

☐ a spacecraft

3. Which can see further?

☐ astronomers' eyes

☐ telescopes

4. Which takes longer to orbit the sun?

☐ Jupiter

☐ Mercury

B Write the right word in each blank. Two words will NOT be used.

astronomers	balloons	cycle	magnetic
orbit	solar	surface	wavelength

Scientists are developing a spacecraft that is powered by steam created by 1. _____ panels. The craft would be like big 2. _____ blown up in space after they are shot up from the earth's 3. _____ by small rockets.

4. _____ have known about sunspots on our solar system's star for a long time. These dark spots are caused by strong 5. _____ fields and occur during a special 6. _____ on the sun.

C Work with a classmate. Talk together about the questions below.

1. What is the name of a famous astronomer?

2. Would you ever want to be an astronaut?

3. What preparations need to be made for a spacecraft to go into space?

4. How does gravity affect a person's weight on different planets?

5. What is something you have seen through a telescope?

D Match the similar words and phrases.

astronaut	explorer	force	gravity	top layer	mechanical person
planets	robot	rocket	solar system	spacecraft	surface

1. _____ and _____   4. _____ and _____

2. _____ and _____   5. _____ and _____

3. _____ and _____   6. _____ and _____

Proper Nouns to Know

Study these words that you will find in the readings for this chapter.

Earth	Galileo	Jupiter	Mars	NASA

Earth's Moon

That huge object orbiting Earth is called the moon. It never needed another name because for a long time people thought it was the only moon in the sky. But that changed when Galileo discovered the moons of Jupiter in 1610. Even without a name, the moon is very interesting. It also does something important for us here on Earth.

The moon is about one fourth the size of Earth. It is also almost 400,000 km away from us. It moves a few centimeters further away each year. A complete orbit of the moon around Earth takes twenty-seven days. One strange thing about our moon is that it spins around at the same rate that it travels around Earth. That is, in those twenty-seven days, the moon turns its face only once. That is why we always see the same side of the moon.

No one knows how the moon came to be in orbit around Earth. The best guess by scientists is that Earth was hit by another object many millions of years ago. The object, they think, was about the size of Mars. At first, they say, the moon was just a giant ball of melted rock. Later, it became hard, with a center that had a lot of metal.

The gases on the surface of the moon are very thin, so space rocks do not burn up as they do on Earth. In fact, they leave some very large holes. One of those holes is more than eighty kilometers wide.

The gravity on the moon is only about one sixth that of Earth. A person who is sixty kilograms on Earth would only be ten kilograms on the moon. The moon's gravity also does something for us here on Earth. Earth does not spin around in a fixed way, and the gravity of the moon controls how much Earth's spinning changes over time. The effect of that control is that our climate does not change so quickly.

The moon is certainly interesting to study. And it is something that will always hold our interest because it is our own moon.

Word Count   350 words

Time

Comprehension Questions

Circle the right answer.

1. This reading is about
    a. man's visits to the moon.
    b. how the moon affects the oceans.
    c. interesting facts about the moon.

2. Which of the following is NOT true?
    a. The moon spins around once every twenty-seven days.
    b. The moon is moving away from Earth.
    c. The moon is older than Earth.

3. According to the writer, the moon has no name because
    a. people thought there was only one moon.
    b. people thought that "Moon" was its name.
    c. people didn't care about giving it a name.

4. Scientists believe that the moon was formed
    a. by a volcano.
    b. by a giant object hitting Earth.
    c. by space rocks.

5. What change is the moon experiencing?
    a. It is spinning faster.
    b. It is getting bigger.
    c. It is moving farther away.

Score _____

Extra Practice

Choose the word or phrase with a similar meaning as the underlined part.

1. The moon orbits Earth.   goes around / surface
2. Galileo discovered Jupiter's moons.   spins / found
3. Space rocks can leave large holes on the surface of the moon.   thin gases / empty places
4. The moon orbits Earth and spins at the same rate.   speed / control
5. The force pulling down is less on the moon than on Earth.   Gravity / Center

Our Star, the Sun

The sun is a giant star that is almost perfectly round. Although the sun spins, it does not spin like a planet does. The middle part of the sun goes faster than the top and bottom of the sun. This is because the sun is made from gas. The middle part of the sun makes a complete turn every 24 days. The bottom and top parts make a complete turn every 35
5 days.

The sun gives off light, and this light is very important to Earth. Not only does this light help living things grow, but the sunlight and heat help make the weather. However, not all of the sunlight can be seen with the eye. There are three parts to sunlight, and the part of light that you can see is only a small piece of that light. The other two parts cannot
10 be seen by the eye but still have important effects on Earth. Most of the energy from the sun comes in the form of light with a long wavelength, longer than red light's wavelength. This part of light is heat.

The sun creates a magnetic field, which has a strong effect on everything around it. Sometimes, there are dark spots, or sunspots, on the sun. Sunspots are caused by the sun's
15 magnetic field. The sun's magnetic field is strong, but sunspots have a magnetic field that is much stronger. Some sunspots have magnetic fields that are about 100 times stronger than the sun's normal magnetic field. Sunspots are cooler than the rest of the sun, but they do not last very long. Sunspots occur during a special cycle on the sun that goes on for 11 years, but sunspots themselves
20 do not last for 11 years. While most of these spots last only a few hours, a few can last for months. Sunspots usually occur when the sun suddenly gives off a lot of energy into space in a certain area, and they can have a big effect on Earth. They can cause problems for cell
25 phones and make the power go out in certain areas.

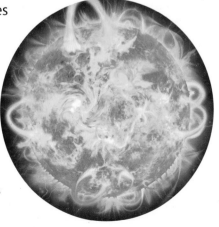

Word Count 350 words

 Time

Comprehension Questions

Circle the right answer.

1. This reading is about
   a. the way the sun helps Earth.
   b. the sun, its light, and its magnetic field.
   c. the kind of material that makes up the sun.

2. The writer says that the sun spins differently from a planet because
   a. of its large, strong magnetic field.
   b. there are different parts of sunlight.
   c. it is made from gas.

3. Which of the following is NOT mentioned about the light from the sun?
   a. It carries the energy from the sun.
   b. Most of it cannot be seen by the eye.
   c. The light we cannot see does not affect Earth.

4. Sunspots can be a problem because
   a. they are cooler than the rest of the sun.
   b. they affect things on Earth.
   c. they have no magnetic field.

5. Sunspots
   a. last for 11 years and are part of a cycle.
   b. are caused by the sun's magnetic field.
   c. cannot be seen by the human eye.

 Score _____

Extra Practice

Write the right word in each blank to complete the summary.

gases	sunspots	magnetic	planet	areas

    The sun is actually a big star made up of 1. _____ . The sun provides light and heat for the 2. _____ Earth. The sun also creates a strong 3. _____ field that affects everything around it. Sometimes this causes 4. _____ on the sun. The 5. _____ in which these occur are cooler and look darker. Though sunspots only last up to a few months, they can cause problems on Earth.

Living on Mars

Some scientists believe that Mars is the planet with the highest chance of supporting human life away from Earth. Of these scientists, some believe that it is possible for humans to reach Mars by 2030. However, there are many questions to answer and things to prepare before this can happen. Scientists must research Mars as well as develop the technology

5 for a person to live safely there. Recently, scientists have sent robots to Mars to gather information about the planet to answer such questions. Is there life on Mars? What is the climate like? What does the land look like? What would be needed for humans to explore Mars?

Putting people on Mars will include planning how a person will live on Mars. At its

10 shortest distance, Mars is 225 million kilometers away from Earth. So, it would take about 6 months for a one-way trip to get there. The planets are moving around the sun at different rates, though. So, astronauts would have to remain on Mars for over 18 months before Earth and Mars were at their closest distance again. Therefore, planning for such a long trip to Mars would include figuring out how much food and supplies would be needed for over

15 two years in space and how such things would be carried.

Astronauts would need to prepare both their minds and bodies for such a long trip away from Earth. NASA set up a special research building in Hawaii that copied the conditions of living on Mars. A group of astronauts stayed in this research building for 366 days. During their stay, they had to deal with what they might have to deal with on Mars.

20 For example, they had to eat bad food. They had to live with each other in a very small space. They also had to deal with the problem of having lots of time with little or nothing to do. They could not receive help from people on the outside for the whole time they were inside. But it is all part of the plan for

25 preparing to put people on Mars one day.

Word Count 350 words

 Time

Comprehension Questions

Circle the right answer.

1. This reading is about
   a. what is necessary to make a journey to Mars.
   b. robots on Mars.
   c. living things that were found on Mars.

2. How long would people have to stay on Mars?
   a. At least a week
   b. About one and a half years
   c. More than twenty years

3. What is a question that scientists will need to research further?
   a. How far away is Mars?
   b. How big is Mars?
   c. What is needed to support human life on Mars?

4. Which of the following is NOT mentioned as part of preparing for a trip to Mars?
   a. Improving technology
   b. Preparing the minds and bodies of astronauts
   c. Finding volunteer astronauts

5. Where was the special research area that copied the conditions of Mars?
   a. On the moon
   b. In Hawaii
   c. In a NASA spacecraft

 Score _____

Extra Practice

Choose the word or phrase with a similar meaning as the underlined part.

1. <u>Astronauts</u> have never been to Mars.   Space explorers / Ships

2. It would take at least six months to <u>reach</u> Mars in a shuttle.   start for / arrive at

3. There are many things to <u>prepare</u> to make a trip to Mars possible.   get ready / explore

4. It is not always easy to <u>deal with</u> people.   get along with / make up

5. The living <u>conditions</u> on Mars will not be the best.   technology / situation

An Eye on Other Planets

There are actually many planets that are outside of our solar system. The first of these far-off planets was discovered in 1988. Since then, astronomers have found more than 3,500 such planets, and they think there are a lot more. Astronomers have found many of them using a special space telescope. This telescope can see very far into space.

5   Many of these planets go around their own star, just like our planet goes around the sun. A few of these planets even go around two stars. However, some of these planets are by themselves and do not go around a star. Astronomers cannot see these planets with their eyes. Instead, they use some special methods to find out where the planets are and what they are like.

10   Even though these planets are very far away from us, we know some things about the planets. We know that they come in all kinds of colors and sizes. Some of the planets appear to be red or blue, and they can be much bigger than Jupiter. Some of these planets also seem to be made of the same kinds of things as can be found on Earth. A number of the far-off planets seem to be completely solid and made of rocks, but astronomers found

15   one that is covered in water. Some of the planets are a little like planets in our own solar system. Astronomers think that a few of the planets seem to have volcanoes. One kind of planet is called a "hot Jupiter." These planets seem to be like Jupiter but are closer to a star than Jupiter is. Because they are closer to their star, they are hotter than Jupiter, too.

While far-off planets are interesting, there is an
20   important reason why astronomers are looking at them. Astronomers want to find a planet like Earth. They think that there may be some out there that have air and water like Earth. Such planets, astronomers believe, may also support life on them. That would certainly be something
25   to find! So astronomers keep searching. Who knows what they will find out there?

Time

Word Count   350 words

Comprehension Questions

Circle the right answer.

1. This reading is about
    a. what far-off planets are like and why we look for them.
    b. the discovery of the first far-off planets and Earth-like planets.
    c. why hot Jupiters are far-off planets and water-filled planets.

2. The writer says that no one has seen far-off planets, but astronomers
    a. have found only a few planets.
    b. have used a space ship to research them.
    c. use special methods to learn about them.

3. Which of the following is NOT mentioned as something found on a far-off planet?
    a. Air and water
    b. Hard rocks
    c. Volcanoes

4. The writer says that astronomers look for far-off planets because
    a. it is interesting and shows us how different the planets can be.
    b. they want to find another planet that is like ours.
    c. some of the telescopes can be used to look deep into space.

5. Hot Jupiters are an example of how far-off planets
    a. are similar to the planets in our solar system.
    b. can be understood by using special methods.
    c. are able to have volcanoes, just like Earth.

Score _____

Extra Practice

Write the right word in each blank to complete the summary.

search	planets	telescopes	astronomers	solar system

Scientists have discovered planets outside of our 1. _____. Some of these 2. _____ orbit stars; others do not. Since all of them are very far away, they must be seen with special 3. _____. 4. _____ think there could be another planet like Earth with life on it. However, they have not found one yet, so they continue to 5. _____.

Water Power for Space Travel

In the future, people may travel to Mars by spacecraft powered by water! The spacecraft in use today are fine for getting things into space, but they are not so good at traveling long distances. These spacecraft burn chemical fuels, and they are very expensive. Scientists say that a water-powered spacecraft could make the trip to Mars at a
5 much lower cost. The idea is just in the planning stages at the moment, but scientists think such a spacecraft could be developed soon.

The key to the water-powered spacecraft is the engine. Regular engines push spacecraft by burning fuel. The water engine will use steam. The steam will be created by solar panels that heat water to a high temperature. Of course, the spacecraft will have to
10 carry a lot of water for the long trip to Mars. Today's spacecraft could not carry that much water. But scientists think that a spacecraft blown up like a balloon will be able to.

One US company has already developed a spacecraft like this. These spacecraft are made of a strong material that is something like the material used for making clothes. Two of them have already been sent up into space. They were sent up using rockets and then
15 later filled with air. "Balloon" spacecraft could be very large and carry enough water for a long trip. Current spacecraft carry a very limited supply of water that has to be used carefully. With a spacecraft that is blown up like a balloon in space, enough water could be carried to power the engines and grow food during the trip.
20 And the people on the spacecraft might even get to take a hot bath!

Scientists say the biggest benefit of such a spacecraft would be cost. A spacecraft that blows up like a balloon and uses water to push it through space would cost about one thirtieth of a normal spacecraft. Such savings naturally
25 encourage continued research into balloon spacecraft and water engines. If these scientists are correct, we may soon be on our way to Mars in a spacecraft powered by water.

Word Count 350 words

Time

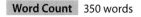

Comprehension Questions

Circle the right answer.

1. This reading is about
   - a. using steam to power a spacecraft.
   - b. going to Mars by balloon.
   - c. the problems in traveling to Mars.

2. Which of these is NOT true of water-powered spacecraft?
   - a. They need to be larger than normal spacecraft.
   - b. They will be like large balloons.
   - c. They cost more than normal spacecraft.

3. The writer says that water-powered spacecraft
   - a. are a long way from being developed.
   - b. are about one thirtieth of the cost of a normal spacecraft.
   - c. can get water from Mars.

4. Besides taking a bath, what else can the astronauts do with the extra water?
   - a. Freeze dangerous things
   - b. Change the surface of Mars
   - c. Grow food

5. Why are spacecraft that can be blown up better for traveling to Mars?
   - a. They can carry a lot of water.
   - b. They are easy to fix if they break.
   - c. They can be blown up on the ground.

 Score _____

Extra Practice

Choose the word or phrase with a similar meaning as the underlined part.

1. Trips to space are expensive because of the <u>long way to travel</u>.　　distance / benefit

2. <u>Spacecraft</u> use a lot of chemical fuel which is expensive.　　Supplies / Rockets

3. Fuel is burned at a very high <u>temperature</u>.　　degree / hot

4. When heated, water turns to <u>steam</u>.　　liquid / gas

5. A spacecraft that runs on steam is only in the planning stage <u>at the moment</u>.　　currently / carefully

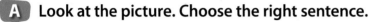

Chapter **8** People

A Look at the picture. Choose the right sentence.

1.

   a. The animal is competing in a surfing contest.

   b. The dog is missing a leg, but it can balance well.

2.

   a. None of the girls look identical to each other.

   b. The mother has passed down her genes for red hair to her children.

3.

   a. These people are wearing the clothes of their country's military forces.

   b. The people want their political leaders to know their opinion.

4.

   a. Today, the girl is celebrating her quinceañera.

   b. Many people have come to the wedding ceremony.

B **What do you think is the right answer to the question? Circle the right choice.**

1.	What do you have when you make your own choices?	Balance	Independence
2.	How might you measure the size of a shark?	In meters	In kilometers
3.	What might a person use instead of a rope?	Boat paddles	Jungle vines
4.	Who fights for a country in a war?	Military forces	Political leaders
5.	What do many children enter at 18?	Adulthood	Childhood

C **Work with a classmate. Ask the questions below and write his/her answers. Then share the answers with the class.**

1. Who in your family has served in the military? _____

2. What is a ceremony you have taken part in? _____

3. What kind of athletic competition have you participated in? _____

4. Are there any twins among your relatives? Are they identical? _____

5. If you had to read a biography of a scientist, who would you want to read about? _____

D **Match the phrases to the right examples.**

1. Famous people in politics _____

2. Coming-of-age traditions _____

3. Famous female surfers _____

4. Scientists of the 20th century _____

5. Things children get from parents _____

6. Asian countries _____

a. quinceañera, sweet 16, bar mitzvah

b. Einstein, Curie, Pavlov

c. Churchill, Kennedy, Gorbachev

d. Myanmar, Japan, Kazakhstan

e. language, faith, political party

f. Bethany Hamilton, Kelly Slater

Proper Nouns to Know

Study these words that you will find in the readings for this chapter.

Albert Einstein	Aung San Suu Kyi	Bethany Hamilton
Burma/Myanmar	Central America	January
National League of Democracy (NLD)	Seijin no Hi	Vanuatu

How to Succeed in Surfing

Bethany Hamilton grew up in Hawaii as the youngest in a family who loved to surf. In 1998, as an 8-year-old girl, she won her first surfing competition. In 2002, she placed first again! She was proving to be one of the top young surfers in the surfing world. However, when she was just 13 years old, Bethany was attacked by a shark, which took her left arm.

5 Luckily, doctors were able to save the young surfer, and she survived.

About twenty shark attacks occur in the US every year. It is a very scary experience if you ask any of those who were attacked and lived to tell. In fact, those attacked and even those who just hear about the shark attacks are scared to enter the water again. That was not the case for Bethany. She loved the ocean and surfing too much to stop. Just a month

10 after the shark attack, she decided she wanted to surf again. But it was not easy. It was harder to swim and move through the water with one arm. It was also hard to balance on the board with one arm. But she was determined to learn how to surf again with one arm. And very soon, she did it!

Just three months after the shark attack, Bethany entered a major surfing

15 competition. This time, she got fifth place. That was not bad at all for someone who had to learn how to surf again. However, Bethany knew that she could do better—and sure enough, she placed first one year later.

Bethany continues to compete in surfing competitions even today, and people are amazed by how successful she has been in the surfing world even after losing one arm.

20 However, Bethany's story is not so much about her talent as it is about her strong will and hard work to be a great surfer after the attack. She continues to prove to herself and others that where there is a will, there is a way. This kind of positive thinking is what makes other people continue to

25 look up to Bethany Hamilton.

Word Count 350 words

Time

Circle the right answer.

1. This reading is about

   a. a teacher who did not give up.

   b. an athlete who is an example to others.

   c. how to find good places to surf.

2. The writer says that Bethany Hamilton won her first competition when she was

   a. 8 years old.

   b. 18 years old.

   c. 30 years old.

3. How did Bethany lose her arm?

   a. Doctors had to remove it.

   b. She was born without it.

   c. A shark bit it.

4. Which is NOT mentioned as something Bethany did after the shark attack?

   a. Give up

   b. Win a competition

   c. Learn to surf again

5. According to the writer, what makes people look up to Hamilton?

   a. Her teaching ability and beauty

   b. Her support for her family

   c. Her talent and strong will

Score _____

Extra Practice

Write the right word in each blank to complete the summary.

competitions	surfer	positive	shark	survived

Bethany Hamilton is a famous 1. _____. When she was younger, her arm was bitten off by a 2. _____. Bethany 3. _____ the attack, but she had to relearn how to surf. Her hard work paid off, and she returned to surfing in 4. _____ just a few months after the attack. Bethany continues to inspire people with her 5. _____ thinking even when things are difficult.

Coming-of-Age Traditions

The age at which a child is considered an adult is different from culture to culture. And many cultures have made different ways to show and celebrate a child's moving into adulthood whenever this happens.

5 In the small island nation of Vanuatu, boys as young as seven jump from a tall tower, which they are tied to by their feet. A boy's feet are tied using a vine. Usually, the boy's mom will hold a toy or something from the boy's childhood. After the jump, it is thrown away. Since a vine is used for the jump, it can be very dangerous. As the boy grows older, he will continue to jump as a way to show that he has the brave heart of a man.

In South and Central America, a special party—called the quinceañera—celebrates
10 a girl turning into a woman at the age of 15. Long ago, the 15th birthday marked a time when a girl would be prepared and ready for marriage. The family would throw a party to allow for the girl to meet possible marriage partners. Today, marriage is not so much the purpose; however, the tradition has continued. The celebration starts with a religious ceremony followed by a big party with lots of food and dancing.

15 In Japan, a person is considered to be an adult at age 20. The "Seijin no Hi" is a festival in January to celebrate the new adults. Those who are 20 years of age at the time dress up in expensive clothes for this festival.

In the United States, some families choose to celebrate a child's 16th birthday or "sweet sixteen" with a big party. However, it is not a tradition that all people celebrate in
20 the US. Instead, 16 is thought to be more important because it is the age at which a person can drive a car after passing a driving test. In a sense, being an adult means having new independence.

Whatever traditions may exist, the time when a young person goes from childhood to adulthood is an
25 important one in almost every culture.

Word Count   350 words

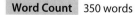
Time _____

Circle the right answer.

1. This reading is about
    a. ways to celebrate becoming an adult.
    b. cultural differences across the US.
    c. how birthdays are celebrated.

2. The writer says that coming of age is
    a. when a child leaves his or her parents' home.
    b. when a child learns how to drive.
    c. when a child is considered an adult by society.

3. The quinceañera is celebrated in
    a. Japan.
    b. South and Central America.
    c. Vanuatu.

4. The Seijin-no-Hi festival in Japan celebrates those who are
    a. seven years old.
    b. fifteen years old.
    c. twenty years old.

5. Age sixteen in the US is seen as a sign of adulthood because
    a. young people go to college at that age.
    b. young people start to work at that age.
    c. young people can drive by law at that age.

 Score _____

Extra Practice

Choose the word or phrase with a similar meaning as the underlined part.

1. Traditions and celebrations are important in every culture. Customs / Vines

2. Cultures consider people to be adults at different ages. think / celebrate

3. Some coming-of-age parties include a religious ceremony. childhood / spiritual

4. Adulthood often comes with increased independence. young / freedom

5. The purpose of a quinceañera is not marriage. to wed / to drive

Twin Studies

If a child has brown hair and blue eyes, one or both of the child's parents probably has brown hair and blue eyes. Why? Genes. Scientists know that the way people look is passed down from parent to child by information in genes. But how about other things? If a parent is shy, then would the child also be shy? If a parent is smart, then will the child also
5 be smart? Scientists want to know how much of who a person is comes from genes. How much of who a person is comes from the way they are raised?

One way scientists have studied this question is by studying identical twins who were separated at birth. Identical twins are twins that look the same on the outside. They also have the same genes on the inside. This is how scientists study their nature. Many
10 years ago, when twins were given away to other families at birth, they didn't always go to the same family. So, they were separated and raised in different ways. This was of great interest to scientists. Even if the twins had the same genes and looked the same, did they turn out the same as adults?

For some things, such as looks or diseases, the twins turned out the same. Even if
15 one twin drank lots of milk and the other did not, they were similar heights as adults. Even if one twin exercised and ate healthy food and the other did not, they could get the same disease as adults. Scientists found that how each twin was raised could not change much.

However, in the case of personality, the answer is not so clear. Some separated twins had completely different
20 personalities and lives as adults. Other separated twins were almost exactly the same. They dressed the same, talked the same, and even had the same jobs—even though they had never met!

In the end, there seems to be no simple answer. As
25 a whole, it seems people become who and what we are because of both genes and how we are raised.

Time

Word Count 350 words

Comprehension Questions

Circle the right answer.

1. This reading is about
   a. whether who we are is a result of genes or of environment.
   b. what genes are and how they work.
   c. how children follow their parents' decisions.

2. The writer says that the way a person physically looks is
   a. something that no one can guess.
   b. determined by what the parents want.
   c. passed down from parent to child.

3. Scientists were interested in studying identical twins
   a. with genes that were very different from their parents.
   b. who were separated and raised in different families.
   c. who both had very strong personalities.

4. Identical twins who do not have the same diet growing up
   a. will grow to be different heights when they are older.
   b. are hard to find because twins usually like the same foods.
   c. may have the same diseases as adults.

5. Which of the following does the writer say is probably true?
   a. Genes and how we are raised make us who we are.
   b. We become who we are mostly because of our genes.
   c. The people we become depends on how we were raised.

 Score _____

Extra Practice

Write the right word in each blank to complete the summary.

diseases	twins	separated	adults	exactly

Identical 1. _____ have the same exact genes. So, they look 2. _____ the same. Identical twins who are 3. _____ at birth have the same genes, but they are raised differently. Scientists study them to learn how similar or how different these twins become as 4. _____ . Scientists found out that genes are usually responsible for 5. _____ , but the way people turn out is often a combination of genes and how kids are raised.

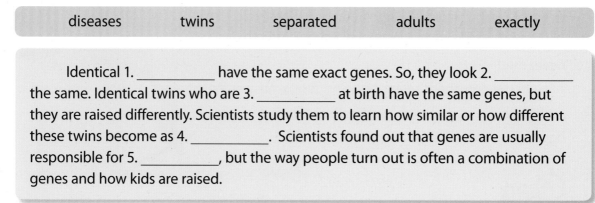

Wonder, Study, and Learn!

A famous scientist once said, "I have no special talent. I am only passionately curious." These words were spoken by none other than Albert Einstein. These words along with other famous sayings by Einstein tell us a lot about the kind of man and researcher he was. For instance, it seems that Einstein did not think of himself as a very smart man. He only

5   thought of himself as a man who was interested in nature and the world around him. One of his famous sayings that help us see the passion he had for studying nature was this: "He who can no longer pause to wonder and stand caught up in awe is as good as dead; his eyes are closed."

Not only was Einstein curious, but he was

10   also a man who loved learning. For him, education did not stop when a person left school. It was something that went on all through life. In his own words, Einstein said, "Intellectual growth should start at birth and stop only at death." He thought

> "We cannot solve our problems with the same thinking we used when we created them."
> Albert Einstein

15   that people should always be learning and growing in their understanding of why things are the way they are. But this learning from nature was not just to know more. Einstein believed that by learning about the world, one would know how to live better. He said, "Look deep into nature, and then you will understand everything better." Einstein also saw the value in the process of learning. It is true that the

20   end result of knowing a fact may have some benefit. However, about the search to know it, Einstein said, "The search for truth is more precious than its possession."

Einstein believed that a person should put one's whole heart into his or her work. And he did just that. By the time he died at 76, his passion for discovering more about the world led him to write hundreds of books and scientific papers. Clearly, he was a man

25   who lived by his own words: "Learn from yesterday, live for today, hope for tomorrow. The important thing is not to stop questioning."

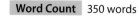
Time

Word Count 350 words

Comprehension Questions

Circle the right answer.

1. This reading is about
   a. Albert Einstein's ideas about life.
   b. Albert Einstein's history.
   c. Albert Einstein's scientific discoveries.

2. The writer says that Albert Einstein's words tell us about
   a. his family.
   b. his work.
   c. his personality.

3. Albert Einstein believed that a person should
   a. learn until high school.
   b. learn until university.
   c. never stop learning.

4. Albert Einstein said that knowing a fact is good, but even better is
   a. the process of learning.
   b. spending time alone in nature.
   c. using that fact to make something new.

5. Which of the following is NOT mentioned about Albert Einstein?
   a. He was curious.
   b. He loved learning.
   c. He was very religious.

 Score _____

Extra Practice

Choose the word or phrase with a similar meaning as the underlined part.

1. Learning starts from <u>the day one is born</u>.   possession / birth

2. A child looks at the stars in <u>wonder</u>.   curious / awe

3. The process of learning is more important than the <u>result</u>.   end / start

4. <u>Passion</u> for learning makes life more exciting.   Growth / Love

5. Children are often <u>curious</u> about nature and animals.   interested / precious

To Make Her Country Free

In 1988, Aung San Suu Kyi went home to Myanmar to visit her sick mother. She left behind her British husband and two sons in England. That trip would change her life.

A military government was in control of Myanmar at the
5   time, and the country was very poor. The people of Myanmar wanted new leaders. When they began to organize meetings and speak against the government in August of 1988, thousands of them were killed. Then Suu Kyi stood up against the government and became a leader of the people. She helped start the National League for Democracy (NLD).

Aung San Suu Kyi had not planned to become a leader in a political fight, but she was
10   the right person for the job. Her father, Aung San, had helped free Myanmar—then named Burma—from British control and was known as "the father of the nation."

In May of 1990, the old military government was voted out of power. Suu Kyi's NLD was chosen by the people to take over. However, the new leaders still wanted the people to have a limited voice in the government. And though Suu Kyi believed in peaceful political change,
15   those now in power knew she was dangerous. So Suu Kyi was locked in her house with police outside. She could not freely come and go.

By now, the whole world was watching Myanmar. Suu Kyi had suddenly become famous around the world. People everywhere were angry and unhappy because of the new government's actions. The military leaders told her she could be free if she left
20   Myanmar, but she refused. She knew she would not be allowed to return if she left. And she wanted to stay and fight for freedom for the people of Myanmar.

For fifteen years, Suu Kyi remained locked in her home in Myanmar. She saw her husband and sons only a few times. Finally, in 2010, she was allowed to go free. The people of Myanmar can never forget Suu Kyi, the woman who gave up her family and her freedom
25   to help make her country free.

Word Count 350 words

Time

Comprehension Questions

Circle the right answer.

1. This reading is about
   a. a woman who worked for freedom in Myanmar.
   b. a man who was the leader of Myanmar.
   c. the mother of Myanmar's president.

2. According to the reading, Suu Kyi
   a. was the daughter of the "father of the nation."
   b. wanted to be the president of Myanmar.
   c. supported the British in Myanmar.

3. The people of Myanmar spoke against the government because
   a. they wanted Suu Kyi as their leader.
   b. they wanted jobs.
   c. they wanted democracy.

4. Which of the following is NOT true about Suu Kyi?
   a. She could not go home to see her family in England.
   b. She was locked in her house for five months.
   c. She helped to start the National League for Democracy.

5. The military government of Myanmar told Suu Kyi she could be free if
   a. she fought against the British.
   b. she became their political leader.
   c. she left the country.

Score _____

Extra Practice

Write the right word in each blank to complete the summary.

voted	military	freedom	lead	government

Myanmar had a 1. _____ government for a long time. However, in 1988 people began to organize and speak against the 2. _____. Eventually, the military government was 3. _____ out. Aung San Suu Kyi had helped to 4. _____ the NLD party to power, but those in power locked her in her house for 15 years. At that time, she chose to give up her 5. _____ and stand for true democracy instead of leaving her country with no chance to return.

Reading Speed Chart

Reading Speed Chart

Write your score for each reading passage at the bottom of the chart. Then put an X in one of the boxes above the reading passage number to mark your time for each passage. Look on the right side of the chart to find your reading speed for each reading passage.

Time																					wpm
1m 30s																					233
1m 35s																					222
1m 40s																					210
1m 45s																					200
1m 50s																					191
1m 55s																					182
2m																					175
2m 5s																					168
2m 10s																					161
2m 15s																					156
2m 20s																					150
2m 25s																					145
2m 30s																					140
2m 35s																					136
2m 40s																					131
2m 45s																					127
2m 50s																					124
2m 55s																					120
3m																					117
3m 5s																					114
3m 10s																					110
3m 15s																					108
Reading	1	2	3	4	5	6	7	8	9	10	11	12	13	14	15	16	17	18	19	20	
Score																					

Reading Speed Chart

Write your score for each reading passage at the bottom of the chart. Then put an X in one of the boxes above the reading passage number to mark your time for each passage. Look on the right side of the chart to find your reading speed for each reading passage.

Time																					wpm
1m 30s																					233
1m 35s																					222
1m 40s																					210
1m 45s																					200
1m 50s																					191
1m 55s																					182
2m																					175
2m 5s																					168
2m 10s																					161
2m 15s																					156
2m 20s																					150
2m 25s																					145
2m 30s																					140
2m 35s																					136
2m 40s																					131
2m 45s																					127
2m 50s																					124
2m 55s																					120
3m																					117
3m 5s																					114
3m 10s																					110
3m 15s																					108
Reading	21	22	23	24	25	26	27	28	29	30	31	32	33	34	35	36	37	38	39	40	
Score																					

How to Use the Apps

Streaming Audio

Step 1: Scan the QR code.

Step 2: Play the track you want to hear.

Track List

Reading 1	Track 1	Reading 11	Track 11	Reading 21	Track 21	Reading 31	Track 31
Reading 2	Track 2	Reading 12	Track 12	Reading 22	Track 22	Reading 32	Track 32
Reading 3	Track 3	Reading 13	Track 13	Reading 23	Track 23	Reading 33	Track 33
Reading 4	Track 4	Reading 14	Track 14	Reading 24	Track 24	Reading 34	Track 34
Reading 5	Track 5	Reading 15	Track 15	Reading 25	Track 25	Reading 35	Track 35
Reading 6	Track 6	Reading 16	Track 16	Reading 26	Track 26	Reading 36	Track 36
Reading 7	Track 7	Reading 17	Track 17	Reading 27	Track 27	Reading 37	Track 37
Reading 8	Track 8	Reading 18	Track 18	Reading 28	Track 28	Reading 38	Track 38
Reading 9	Track 9	Reading 19	Track 19	Reading 29	Track 29	Reading 39	Track 39
Reading 10	Track 10	Reading 20	Track 20	Reading 30	Track 30	Reading 40	Track 40